A Closer Walk with Him

SheLovesGod.com
Study Lessons
Volume 1

by Marnie L. Pehrson

Published by CES Business Consultants
514 Old Hickory Ln * Ringgold GA 30736
Tel: 706-866-2295
www.SheLovesGod.com

Printed in the United States of America

ISBN: 0-9729750-3-9

*Dedicated to the wonderful readers
and contributors at SheLovesGod.com who
strive to center their lives on the Savior and
seek to follow Him in word and deed.*

How to Read This Book

There are 52 lessons within this volume. You can read them in any order or you can work through them one lesson each week for the course of a year. They are generally arranged in order from January through December.

Table of Contents

Prove Me Now Herewith

Do you struggle with making ends meet? Do you wrestle with debt or need help with managing your money wisely? The Lord has a solution!

Most of the time when we read Malachi 3:8-11 we think of the law of tithing and how the Lord promises to open the windows of heaven for our sake when we are honest with Him and give Him ten percent of our increase. Tithing is a principle I've been taught and practiced since childhood. I've found that paying tithing has blessed me with the things I need when I needed them. We may scrape by financially but somehow the money we need appears when we need it most or we'll be given the wisdom to get by on what we have. The windows of heaven have opened for me spiritually and physically in knowledge, wisdom and understanding.

But I'll be honest with you, I'm not the best money manager in the world and monetarily-speaking I don't know that you could say that the windows of heaven have poured me out more money than I could receive! We've struggled a lot with debt in our married life. Perhaps you know what it's like when it feels like every dollar you earn is already earmarked by the interest monster. Or maybe you know what it's like when no matter how much you make, you still manage to spend it all. Getting out of debt and managing our money wisely has been a heightened concern for me over the last year. I've felt an urgency to get out of debt and have made it a matter of prayer and fasting and the Lord has repeatedly opened the windows of heaven and given me insights and hope.

Then, three months ago while listening to a lesson at church I heard a powerful principle taught which I'd either never heard or never paid attention to before. Perhaps I wasn't ready to receive it until that particular Sunday morning when it hit me with such force that I decided to test it. Before I tell you this principle, let's take a look at Malachi 3:8-11 because it's in here... I just never noticed it before.

"Will a man rob God? Yet ye have robbed me. But ye say, Wherein have we robbed thee? In tithes and offerings. Ye are cursed with a curse: for ye have robbed me, even this whole nation.

"Bring ye all the tithes into the storehouse, that there may be meat in mine house, and prove me now herewith, saith the LORD of hosts, if I will not open you the windows of heaven, and pour you out a blessing, that there shall not be room enough to receive it.

"And I will rebuke the devourer for your sakes, and he shall not destroy the fruits of your ground; neither shall your vine cast her fruit before the time in the field, saith the LORD of hosts" (Malachi 3:8-11).

Most of the time when we read this passage we think of tithing – that ten percent. But He says we rob God when we do not give tithes AND offerings. Offerings are over and above the 10 percent. While tithing is generally what we give to our church to help it function and provide the building, facilities, utilities, etc to operate, our offerings are over and above the ten percent and would go toward other charitable causes like feeding the hungry, clothing the naked, healing the sick, supporting missionaries, helping the needy obtain education, etc.

I believe that the windows of heaven are not fully opened until we address both tithes AND offerings. If we really want to have showered upon us so much that we cannot receive it, then we must be generous in our offerings as well. I realize this can be hard to do when you're still struggling with the tithing principle, but it is one of those tests of faith that Jesus spoke of when he said, "If any man will do his will, he shall know of the doctrine" (John 7:17).

Malachi 3 is one of the few places in scripture where the Lord says "prove me." In other words, *test me, try me, and see if I don't do it.* When I heard this, I decided to put the principle to the test and I've seen amazing results. I've also corroborated these results with a friend who has faithfully paid generous tithes and offerings for years. It has been our experience that whatever we give over and above tithing comes back to us ten-fold – if not more. We looked at what we normally make and compared our increase to the amount we gave in offerings and it was ten times the offerings. For example, if you give a dollar, you get back ten. If you give ten, you get back one-hundred.

It's almost as if the Lord is saying, if you'll give me ten percent of your increase, I'll see that you're taken care of. If you'll give me more, I'll repay you ten-fold. I can't find a scriptural reference to back up this ten-factor, so you'll just have to do as Malachi says and prove the Lord for yourself and see what your own personal multiplier is. But it's definitely worth trying to see how it works for you. It may not come back to you exactly ten-fold, but it will come back to you abundantly. As Melvin J. Ballard once said, "a person cannot give a crust to the Lord without receiving a loaf in return."[1]

I find that as I keep this principle in mind, I'm wiser in my spending because I know that five dollars spent on a frivolous or discretionary item is five dollars less that I'll be able to give to the Lord and about $50 less He'll be able to bless me with. It's helping us not only have the money we need to pay down our debts, but also helping us to be wiser with the money we're given.

If you're anything like me, New Year's resolutions fall by the wayside within a few weeks. This year I'm making only one resolution and I believe it's one I'll be able to stick with. I'm not focusing on getting out of debt or even on spending money more frugally. Neither one of those get me excited or motivate me. No, this year, I'm setting only this one resolution – to daily ask myself, "How much can I give?"

How can I stretch and give more to the Lord spiritually and monetarily? How can I use my talents and resources to build the Kingdom of God? For in so doing, the Lord will rebuke the devourer for my sake and will rain blessings down from heaven. Jesus said, "Give, and it shall be given unto you; good measure, pressed down, and shaken together, and running over, shall men give into your bosom" (Luke 6: 38).

I issue you a challenge to put this principle to the test. Let the Lord prove His faithfulness in your life!

1. Marion G. Romney, "The Blessings of the Fast," Ensign, July 1982, 2

Are You Feeling Overwhelmed?

Do you ever feel overwhelmed by so many options, activities and responsibilities that you lose focus on what's really important in the eternal scheme of things? I do sometimes. A friend of mine says, "If Satan can't make you bad, he'll make you busy." Richard G. Scott put it this way, "Are there so many fascinating, exciting things to do or so many challenges pressing down upon you that it is hard to keep focused on that which is essential? When things of the world crowd in, all too often the wrong things take highest priority. Then it is easy to forget the fundamental purpose of life. Satan has a powerful tool to use against good people. It is distraction. He would have good people fill life with 'good things' so there is no room for the essential ones. Have you unconsciously been caught in that trap?" [1]

What can you do when this happens? When I start feeling overwhelmed, discouraged or experience a lack of vision, I take time to reevaluate my priorities, because typically when I'm feeling this way it's because my priorities have shifted out of order. Psalms 119:133 says, *"Order my steps in thy word: and let not any iniquity have dominion over me."*

This verse gives us some guidelines to follow on how to order our priorities. It prompts us to ask ourselves a series of important questions.

Am I prayerfully studying God's Word every day?

The psalmist recognized that the Word of God helps us order our priorities. When we daily study God's word, we put ourselves in tune with His Spirit. Answers and guidance that we need on a daily basis can then be communicated to us more readily because we'll be in tune with the Spirit of God. I like to think of the way the Holy Spirit communicates with us as tuning into a channel. When we prayerfully study God's word, we put our spirits on the right channel to receive direction. Sometimes it comes straight from the pages; other times, the inspiration comes simply because we have put ourselves in tune with the channel the Spirit uses and are in a position to hear the message He's "broadcasting" to us.

Have I slipped back into bad habits?

Ask yourself, "Have I let iniquity or bad habits regain their dominion over me?" This could be anything from slipping back into past sins, giving in to enslaving addictions or simply putting other things in the place of God in our hearts.

What are my life-long and eternal goals?

Decide or reaffirm what you want to accomplish with your life and what treasures you'd like to lay up for eternity? (See Matthew 6:19-20) Write it down. Make it yours. Remember that you can't take that car or house with you beyond the grave. But you can take the knowledge and wisdom you gain here. And you can take those you love along with you.

Where am I spending my time?

What dominates your thoughts and the use of your time? Jesus said, "Seek ye first the kingdom of God and His righteousness and all these things shall be added unto you" (Matthew 6:33). Make a list of all your projects, responsibilities, activities and demands. Now grade them on the following scale:

A = Essential (Eternally Significant)
B = Necessary / Important
C = Worthwhile
D = Unimportant
F = Counterproductive

Am I spending time each day on the essential and eternal things?

Based on the grades you gave your activities and concerns, are you spending time on the things that really matter? Are there activities that are worthwhile, but not necessary or essential? What could you delegate or drop? Are you wasting time on unimportant time wasters or counterproductive concerns that actually take you away from your eternal goals? Could you drop these to free time for more essential and eternally consequential priorities?

It's a good idea to conduct a self-evaluation every month or even each week as you plan out your activities. Especially use this exercise when you're feeling overwhelmed or losing perspective. Prayerfully let the Lord help you set your priorities and plan your months, weeks and even days. I find it very beneficial to start my days with a prayer and specifically ask for guidance on my daily tasks. When I take the time to consult with Heavenly Father and write down what He wants me to do for the day, I am much more productive and focused than if I leave my day to chance or to whatever the mood strikes me to do.

Give it a try and let me know how it works for you. Remember, "The steps of a good man (or woman) are ordered by the Lord: and he delighteth in his way" (Ps. 37: 23). Let the Lord order your steps! You'll be a lot more balanced, successful and happy.

1) Richard G. Scott, "First Things First," *Ensign*, May 2001, 7, 9

Lessons from Creation: Orderly Growth

There is an important principle of order that we can learn from our Creator. It is the principle of orderly growth found in the book of Genesis in the six creative periods. Everything was created logically and in order.

Day 1: Separation of light and darkness
Day 2: Separation of the waters on earth from the water in the atmosphere
Day 3: Creation of earth, seas, and vegetation.
Day 4: Creation of lights — Sun, Moon, Stars, and Seasons
Day 5: Creation of whales, fish, fowls
Day 6: Creation of cattle, beasts, animals, man and woman.

Notice that each day built on the one before. The fish could not be created before the seas. The plants could not be created before the sun and the earth. We too must do things in order. You cannot run before you know how to crawl. In your homes, careers, and even in your spiritual growth, you must do things in wisdom and in order. It is not requisite that you should run faster than you have strength. Getting ahead of yourself and trying to do too many things at once will only serve to overwhelm you.

I believe as women we expect too much from ourselves in many respects, yet often neglect the weightier matters. We expect ourselves to be Super Mom's — these dynamic women with successful careers and healthy, happy and brilliant children, glamorous wives for our husbands, spotless home managers, and spiritual giants. Few of us can live up to these kinds of expectations without cracking under the pressure.

Instead of trying to be everything at once, we can learn to pace ourselves while keeping the important things uppermost in our minds. We can also realize that "To every thing there is a season, and a time to every purpose under the heaven" (Ecclesiastes 3:1). We can have it all as women, but sometimes it may not be possible to have it all simultaneously. There are choices to be made. We might have to sacrifice our spotless house when our babies are little in order to be better mothers or to be able to continue to develop our talents. We might have to put down that career magazine to spend more time with our husband or to read our scriptures.

It is really a matter of priorities. When we put God first in our lives, everything else will naturally fall into place. Matthew 6:33 explains, "But seek ye first the kingdom of God, and his righteousness; and all these things shall be added unto you." When we seek God first and truly hunger and thirst after righteousness (Matt 5:6), we are filled. I speak from experience when I say that if we truly have God first in our lives, but we have the remainder of our priorities out of order, the Lord has a way of making us feel uneasy and off-center until we straighten out the rest of those priorities.

But what are those other priorities? When we put God first, and seek to live our lives in accordance with his will, we learn of Christ's commandment, "A new commandment I give unto you, That ye love one another; as I have loved you, that ye also love one another. By this shall all men know that ye are my disciples, if ye have love one to another" (John 13:34).

Love begins at home — whether in the family we grew up in, the family we have, or the one we hope to have. We learn about love in our families as we serve, teach and spend time with each other. The natural consequence of putting God first in our lives leads us to pull our family to the top of our priorities as well.

Once we have God first in our lives, we are prepared to reach out to others within our circle of influence. We learn that when we are in the service of our fellow beings, we are only in the service of our God. As Christ taught in Matthew 25:40, "Inasmuch as ye have done it unto one of the least of these my brethren, ye have done it unto me."

Once we are clear on what really matters most to us in our lives, choices become easier. When we are forced to let something go because we do not have the time or energy to do everything we'd like to do, we'll know what to keep and what to set aside.

I am not speaking to you about these things because I have them all figured out. This is a daily struggle for me. But I have learned that God will help us change our hearts and shift our priorities. God has blessed me with events and people who have helped me pull Him to the number one spot. And it has totally transformed my life. I still struggle between career and family time, but I am actively working to pull loving and serving my family and others higher up the ladder.

I testify to each of you that Jesus Christ lives — that He is our Savior, our one and only Advocate with the Father. And by

Him, and through Him and of Him the worlds are and were created (John 1:1-3). As James E. Talmage once said, "The world's greatest champion of woman and womanhood is Jesus Christ." He understands the many roles we fill as women and he is waiting and willing to help us with the demands on our time and our energy. He stands ready — waiting to help us if we will but ask. He so wants to shower each of us with his blessings. As we put Him first in our lives, He will "open the windows of heaven, and pour out a blessing, that there shall not be room enough to receive it" (Malachi 3:10). Of this I testify in the name of Jesus Christ.

Self-Confidence Is
Not the Answer

Among people today there seems to be an epidemic of low self-esteem, low self-confidence. For decades self-help books have been promoting ideas such as affirmations (positive self-talk) and other methods as a means of building one's self-esteem. For example, an overweight, timid woman might be admonished to begin every morning by standing in front of the mirror and saying, "I am a thin, beautiful, confident woman." Supposedly, if she says this enough, she'll become this person. But does she really believe this? Can she look in the mirror and feel like she's being honest with herself? Hardly. Not only does she doubt this statement, but she also feels like a liar.

I recently attended a teleclass given by Michael Losier at Teleclass International about the Universal Law of Attraction. In this class, Mr. Losier suggested that these types of affirmations be rephrased into something one can feel honest and good about such as, "I am in the process of learning all I need to be, have and do to become a thin, beautiful, confident woman." This kind of statement keeps you honest because you certainly can be in the process of learning. It keeps you motivated toward action (having, being and doing) and keeps your goal in mind. But, most of all you can say this statement without having your mind filled with doubts or disbelief.

There is a direct correlation between the amount of doubt we have in our mind and our ability to achieve or accomplish anything. Doubt and faith cannot dwell in a mind simultaneously. With faith, we can move mountains, but enter even the smallest doubt, and no mountain gets moved.

Which brings me to the point of this article – self-confidence is not the answer. It will never be enough, because no matter how accomplished or knowledgeable we are, there is always room for doubt about ourselves. We're all human. We all make mistakes. When we lean on ourselves, we're leaning on a flawed cane that has the ability to bow, bend and crack with the right amount of pressure or wind. No amount of positive thinking or positive affirmations will ever change the fact that we are fallible.

I am probably one of the most self-confident people you could ever meet. My parents filled me with positive thoughts about myself and made me believe that nothing was impossible for me — that I was smart and capable of achieving anything I set my mind to. But even with all that self-confidence, I know there are things I simply cannot do on my own. And this is where something my mother taught me comes in handy, "Say a little prayer."

I've been in business since 1990, and as I've spent some time contemplating what I have learned over these years, it is this one simple lesson: "Do your best and God will make up the rest." I have no doubt about these three facts:

1. That there is an answer – a way – to accomplish anything;
2. That God knows that answer or that way; and

3.   That when working toward any worthy goal, if I do my
     best to learn, work and ask God for direction, He will
     provide a way or give me the answer.

I cannot count the number of times that my mind has been
blank when I needed to write an article and I got on my knees
and prayed for direction and He gave me not only a topic, but
also the entire article. I cannot enumerate the times I stalled
out with a perplexing programming problem, and when I
asked, the Lord gave me the solution. Nor can I count the
number of times I didn't know where I'd get the money to pay
my electricity or house payment, and I got down on my knees
and ask the Lord to show me a way to earn the money, and He
did. And I didn't have to be perfect and flawless to receive
these answers. My family and close friends can attest to the
fact that I am most definitely an imperfect being.

The combination of unwavering faith in His ability and desire
to help us, along with our own willingness to learn and work
hard is an unstoppable combination. Self-confidence is
worthless when you've hit the impenetrable wall where
mortal answers and mortal capabilities end. But this need not
discourage us, God knows everything and He is willing and
able to share His knowledge with us if we are willing to doubt
Him not, but be believing and come to Him with all our hearts,
willing to work, learn and serve.

I would like to publicly express my gratitude for my Heavenly
Father, who has blessed me beyond measure with wonderful
parents, family, friends and more. I am grateful for a Father in
heaven who hears and answers our prayers and helps us in
spite of our faults, weaknesses and inadequacies. He is more

than capable of compensating for these if we come to Him
with a repentant heart, with a contrite spirit and ask Him in
faith. I am thankful that He has always provided a way —
Jesus Christ is that way, the truth, and the life. (John 14:6) He
created the worlds, He parted the Red Sea; He turned the
water into wine; He healed the lame, the blind, and the leper.
He forgave the woman caught in adultery and conquered the
grave. There is no problem or challenge beyond His ability or
desire to remedy. Never doubt it. Do your best and I promise
you that God *will* most certainly make up the rest.

My Spirit Shall Not Always Strive With Man

One of the greatest challenges we face in our modern age is a propensity to excess. We work to excess, play to excess, or rest in excess. Some people go overboard in the pleasures of the world that lead to sin and bondage, but for others of us who are trying to live the way the Savior taught, Satan can't be quite so bold. Instead, he subtly takes something that is not intrinsically bad – even a strength - and encourages us to carry it to an extreme. He knows that even too much of a good thing can cause great damage in our lives. This could be over involvement in activities, workaholism, spending too much time on a sport or hobby, or wasting too many hours in front of the television. There's nothing wrong with extra curricular activities, working hard, having hobbies or watching some TV, but when they become our obsession, our lives become like a car with one over-inflated tire while the other 3 tires become neglected, low or flat. We're an accident waiting to happen.

Finding balance in our lives is rarely easy – especially if we're the "all or nothing" type of personality. I'm one of these people. Whatever I'm interested in, I tend to focus on it like a laser beam. One of my good friends teases me sometimes and says, "Hey, Marnie, point that laser beam in a different direction, will ya?" If I'm helping, I over-help. If I'm working, I over-work. If I'm learning and teaching spiritual things, I go at it with all my heart. Over the last few years, I've felt like Paul described the house of Stephanas, who had "addicted themselves to the ministry of the saints" (1 Corinthians 16:15).

My addictive personality had addicted itself to the things of
God, and the only side effect to that addiction is pure joy.

But we all live in the world. We have to work, earn a living,
care for our families, and deal with the day-to-day challenges
of life. Over time, I started letting some air out of my spirituality tire. Then last month, there was a career goal that I really
wanted to meet. It was important to me on many levels – for
my family's financial stability and growth, for my own social
and mental growth, etc. It was a challenge I earnestly wanted
to meet. I pursued the goal, reached it and then realized that
in my over-zealousness to attain my objective, I had not
thought about the things that would be required of me as a
result. I quickly found myself working around the clock,
neglecting my family and worst of all, neglecting my spiritual
nourishment.

Sensing the drop from a higher level of spirituality to a lower
one, it didn't take long for me to notice the symptoms of
spiritual malnutrition. These include irritability, stress, a
wandering mind during prayer, inability to find anything
interesting about reading scriptures, and a general lack of
communication from the Spirit. I was shocked to discover that
in a matter of only 2-3 weeks the "oil in one's lamp" could
burn so low. Normally, we think that overt sin is what clogs
our spiritual channels, but I've learned that if we don't
regularly use those channels, our ability to employ them
becomes diminished. They become like a car that's set unused
on your front lawn for so long that it takes forever to start.

As I've become aware of this phenomenon in my own life, I've
made a conscious effort to slow down my work and make time

for spiritual things. As a result, a little more oil gets added to my lamp every day and the spiritual lines of communication begin to function again. I've learned several things from this experience, but first and foremost is best summarized in a little verse that's been running through my mind lately. It's found in Genesis 6:3: "My spirit shall not always strive with man." It's not that the Lord pulls away from us, it's that we pull away from Him. If we compare our ability to communicate with God to a two-way radio, God is still broadcasting on the same channel on which He's always been broadcasting, but we have turned our radio to another channel and He's either coming in fuzzy or not at all.

The second thing I've learned from this is that the longer we neglect our spiritual two-way radio, the longer it takes to find God's channel again. If my radio gets out of tune for a day, it's much easier to find the channel again the next day than if I've waited two or three weeks to correct the problem. If one were to wait months or years, the difficulty in finding a clear communication with God would increase exponentially.

The third lesson is that spiritual oil cannot be stored. Today's spiritual experiences will not enlighten you if you have neglected to fill the oil in your spiritual lamp for months or years. You cannot live on borrowed light – not even your own! Spiritual nourishment is like the manna that fell from heaven for the Israelites to eat in the wilderness. Each day they were to gather only enough for that day – nothing more. If they gathered more, it went bad. Heavenly sustenance is a day-to-day requirement. It builds on itself, but it doesn't store up.

How are your spiritual channels? Are you in tune with the Spirit? Are you receiving daily insight and direction? Are your prayers meaningful? Are you practically applying the scriptures you read on a daily basis to your life? If so, great job! Keep it up and remember to feed your soul daily. If not, then do something about it now before your spiritual radio is so out of tune that it takes a painful experience to help you find God's channel again.

Charity Never Faileth

Many of us think of monetary contributions when we hear the word charity. We may think of giving to the Red Cross, to cancer research, or we may think of millionaires who devote large sums of money to important causes. With this concept of charity, we may think, "Oh, I can't be charitable because I do not have the money or the means to be." But, in reality, charity has very little if anything to do with money.

What is Charity?

The Apostle Paul explained that charity is more than giving, but rather is a state of the heart, "And though I bestow all my goods to feed the poor, and though I give my body to be burned, and have not charity, it profiteth me nothing" (1 Corinthians 13:3).

Charity, as described in the scriptures, is comprised of three dimensions:

1. the perfect love that Jesus has for us,
2. the love that He asks us to have for each other,
3. and the love we should have for Him.

To explain charity a little more clearly, we can take 1 Corinthians 13:4-8 and substitute Jesus for the word charity:

"*Jesus* suffereth long, and is kind; *Jesus* envieth not; *Jesus* vaunteth not *Him*self, is not puffed up, Doth not behave

*Him*self unseemly, seeketh not *His* own, is not easily pro-
voked, thinketh no evil; Rejoiceth not in iniquity, but rejoiceth
in the truth; Beareth all things, believeth all things, hopeth all
things, endureth all things. *Jesus* never faileth… "

Jesus is the embodiment of this pure love. His love resulted
from a life of serving, sacrificing and giving in behalf of
others. Through His agonizing Atonement, the Savior gave us
the ultimate demonstration of love. "Greater love hath no man
than this, that a man lay down his life for his friends" (John
15:13).

Why Do We Need It?

Jesus commanded that we develop and demonstrate this love:
"A new commandment I give unto you, That ye love one
another; as I have loved you, that ye also love one another. By
this shall all men know that ye are my disciples, if ye have
love one to another" (John 13:34-35). When was the last time
that someone recognized you as a Christian simply by the
love and kindness you demonstrated to others?

In Matthew 25, Jesus gave a parable that demonstrates the
importance of possessing this perfect love called charity. He
explains that when He comes again in His glory, He will
gather all the nations and separate the sheep on His right
hand and the goats on His left. Those on the right hand (the
sheep) will be joint-heirs with Him, while those on the left-
hand (the goats) will have no such privileges.

What determines whether you're a sheep or a goat? Charity!
The Savior explained that those on His right hand will be

told, "Come, ye blessed of my Father, inherit the kingdom prepared for you from the foundation of the world: For I was an hungered, and ye gave me meat: I was thirsty, and ye gave me drink: I was a stranger, and ye took me in: Naked, and ye clothed me: I was sick, and ye visited me: I was in prison, and ye came unto me. "

"Then shall the righteous answer him, saying, Lord, when saw we thee an hungered, and fed thee? or thirsty, and gave thee drink? When saw we thee a stranger, and took thee in? or naked, and clothed thee? Or when saw we thee sick, or in prison, and came unto thee?"

And He shall answer, "Verily I say unto you, Inasmuch as ye have done it unto one of the least of these my brethren, ye have done it unto me."

"Then shall He say also unto them on the left hand, Depart from me, ye cursed, into everlasting fire, prepared for the devil and his angels: For I was an hungered, and ye gave me no meat: I was thirsty, and ye gave me no drink: I was a stranger, and ye took me not in: naked, and ye clothed me not: sick, and in prison, and ye visited me not.

Then shall they also answer Him, saying, Lord, when saw we thee an hungered, or athirst, or a stranger, or naked, or sick, or in prison, and did not minister unto thee?

Then shall He answer them, saying, Verily I say unto you, Inasmuch as ye did it not to one of the least of these, ye did it not to me. And these shall go away into everlasting punishment: but the righteous into life eternal" (Matthew 25:31-46).

How Do We Obtain Charity?

The only way for us to develop this Christ-like love is to practice the process outlined by the Master. "Hereby perceive we the love of God, because He laid down His life for us: and we ought to lay down our lives for the brethren" (1 John 3:16).

Although we may never be called to lay down our lives for another, we do have the opportunity to sacrifice and serve others. The process of developing charity by sacrificing for others is most notably demonstrated in motherhood. "Do you know one reason why righteous mothers love their children so much? It is because they sacrifice so much for them. We love what we sacrifice for and we sacrifice for what we love." [1] Through selflessly serving others, we develop Christ-like love for them.

"Charity is not just a precept or a principle, nor is it just a word to describe actions or attitudes. Rather, it is an internal condition that must be developed and experienced in order to be understood. We are possessors of charity when it is a part of our nature. People who have charity have a love for the Savior, have received of His love, and love others as He does." [2]

Charity comes when we give of ourselves — our time and our talents. "[The Savior's] gifts were rare ones: eyes to the blind, ears to the deaf, and legs to the lame; cleanliness to the unclean, wholeness to the infirm, and breath to the lifeless. His gifts were ... forgiveness to the repentant, hope to the despairing. His friends gave Him shelter, food, and love. He gave them of Himself, His love, His service, His life. ... We should strive to give as He gave. To give of oneself is a holy gift." [3]

1) Ezra Taft Benson, *The Teachings of Ezra Taft Benson*, Bookcraft, p. 444
2) C. Max Caldwell, "Love of Christ," *Ensign*, Nov. 1992, 29
3) Spencer W. Kimball, *The Wondrous Gift* [1978], 2.

One Selfless Act
Goes A Long Way

In 1 Kings 17, the Lord sent the prophet Elijah to tell the
wicked king Ahab, "As the Lord God of Israel liveth, before
whom I stand, there shall not be dew nor rain these years, but
according to my word." And then the Lord told Elijah to, "Get
thee hence, and turn thee eastward, and hide thyself by the
brook Cherith, that is before Jordan. And it shall be, that thou
shalt drink of the brook; and I have commanded the ravens to
feed thee there."

So Elijah went according to the word of the Lord. And the
ravens brought him food to eat and he drank from the brook.
After a while the brook dried up, because there had been no
rain in the land. And the word of the Lord came to him,
saying, "Arise, get thee to Zarephath, which belongeth to
Zidon, and dwell there: behold, I have commanded a widow
woman there to sustain thee."

So without questioning Elijah went to Zarephath. When he
came to the gate of the city, the widow woman was there
gathering sticks: and he called to her, and said, "Fetch me, I
pray thee, a little water in a vessel, that I may drink."

As she was going to fetch it, he called to her, and said, "Bring
me, I pray thee, a morsel of bread in thine hand."

But she replied, "As the Lord thy God liveth, I have not a cake,
but an handful of meal in a barrel, and a little oil in a cruse:

and, behold, I am gathering two sticks, that I may go in and dress it for me and my son, that we may eat it, and die."

Elijah answered, "Fear not; go and do as thou hast said: but make me thereof a little cake first, and bring it unto me, and after make for thee and for thy son. For thus saith the Lord God of Israel, The barrel of meal shall not waste, neither shall the cruse of oil fail, until the day that the Lord sendeth rain upon the earth."

She went and did according to the saying of Elijah: and she, and he, and her house, did eat many days. And the barrel of meal wasted not, neither did the cruse of oil fail, according to the word of the Lord, which he spake by Elijah.

The Lord Always Prepares A Way for Obedience

There are some important lessons we can learn from Elijah and the widow. The first is that when the Lord says to do something, we should do it. To his credit, when Elijah was told to go, he went. He didn't waver or equivocate. He simply followed the Lord's instructions and was blessed for it.

The faith exhibited by the widow in her desperate circumstances is among the greatest seen in the Bible. When Elijah asked her to take her last morsel of food and give it to him, she did so – in spite of her fears. Perhaps she thought that even if the food didn't last that at least she and her son would die performing one last act of charity.

We learn from Elijah and the widow that when we do the things that the Lord commands, He always prepares a way for us to accomplish the thing which He has commanded.

The Lord Blesses Us Through Each Other

When the brook ran dry, the Lord told Elijah where to go to obtain food: "I have commanded a widow woman there to sustain thee." The Lord prepared means of survival for Elijah and met his needs through another. Notice the Lord's economy. Through each of their possessions, talents and gifts the widow and Elijah were able to sustain each other. If Elijah had not gone to the widow, she and her son surely would have died. And if Elijah had not been led to this faith-filled widow who was willing to sacrifice her last morsel to help another, then he would have gone hungry.

So many times in our lives we are led to others whom we can help and bless. And in so doing, we ourselves are blessed. The Lord is a master "matchmaker." When we are willing to open ourselves up, reach out to others and even allow them to serve us, great blessings result.

One Selfless Act of Faith & Service Goes a Long Way

Why do you think the widow was asked to make such a difficult sacrifice? Often the greater the sacrifice the greater the reward. Because she was willing to sacrifice one small cake, the Lord blessed her and her son throughout the remainder of the famine. One act of faith can yield great rewards. Because

she had been kind to Elijah, not only were she and her son
fed, but also later on, Elijah even raised her son from the dead.

"When we put God first, all other things fall into their proper
place or drop out of our lives. Our love of the Lord will govern
the claims for our affection, the demands on our time, the
interests we pursue, and the order of our priorities. ... "May
God bless us to put [him] first and, as a result, reap peace in
this life and eternal life with a fullness of joy in the life to
come." [1]

May we each exhibit the courage and faith to follow the
examples of Elijah and the widow. Let us follow the Lord
without question, use our talents and means to selflessly serve
others and as a result become instruments in God's hands to
bless lives. In so doing, the blessings of heaven will flow
down upon us and sustain us in our times of trial.

1) Ezra Taft Benson, Ensign, May 1988, 4, 6.

Faith Is The Stuff
From Which Miracles Are Made

I recently heard a thought-provoking quote, "I am perfectly satisfied that my Father and my God is a cheerful pleasant, lively and good-natured Being. Why? Because I am cheerful, pleasant, lively and good natured when I have His Spirit" (Heber C. Kimball).

That's quite an outstanding observation isn't it — that God is a cheerful, pleasant and good-natured Being? It's a significant contrast from the stern Being sitting on a throne amidst the clouds waiting to zap you with a thunderbolt should you break His commands – isn't it? God does seem to delight in and promote a glad heart. Psalms 32:11 tells us "Be glad in the Lord, and rejoice, ye righteous: and shout for joy, all ye that are upright in heart."

When suffering amidst the consequences of my own poor choices, I've been guilty of approaching my Heavenly Father as if He were a stern, indignant parent who would require me to suffer the full extent of the consequences of my actions. This perspective of my Heavenly Father affected the amount of faith I had that He would truly deliver me. After all, if I pray, "thy will be done" but believe that His character is such that His "will" is that I mercilessly suffer the full extent for the consequences of my actions, then how much faith can I really have in deliverance?

James E. Talmage said, "Faith is of itself a principle of power and by its presence or absence even the Lord was and is influenced and in a great measure controlled in the bestowal or withholding of blessings." Hebrews 11:1 says "Faith is the substance of things hoped for, the evidence of things not seen." If faith is the stuff from which miracles are made then my perspective of God's personality and character could actually affect the outcome of my prayers!

We sometimes question who qualifies for God's deliverance. God delivered the Children of Israel who, through no fault of their own, suffered 400 years in Egyptian bondage. He parted the Red Sea for them, but will He part the Red Sea for someone who brought her calamity upon herself? Upon studying the cycles of the children of Israel in the book of Judges, it's evident that God does indeed deliver the foolish from their own sins and poor choices. In the book of Judges, the children of Israel follow this cycle:

· They would forsake the Lord, pick up the bad habits and idol worship of their neighbors.
· They would lose the Lord's Spirit and protection because they no longer served Him.
· Left to themselves, they would suffer the consequences of their actions and become enslaved to a neighboring nation.
· In their bondage, they would be brought down into the depths of humility.
· They would cry to the Lord for deliverance.
· The Lord would send them a judge to deliver them.
· They would rejoice and serve the Lord until the judge died.
· Once the judge died they would forsake the Lord and the cycle would start over.

Personally, I believe God allows us to suffer through the consequences of our poor choices long enough for us to learn what we need to learn from the situation. We may need to learn patience, trust, faith or how to relinquish control. But I do believe deliverance will come. Perhaps we only have to stay in the mire of bondage until we develop faith enough to enable the miracle? This all sounds good on paper, of course. It's easy to tell others to stay strong and have faith that the Lord will deliver them. But I've found that when it's me that needs rescuing, then it's much more difficult to have faith and believe that God isn't going to make me pay the "uttermost farthing" for my mistakes. Somehow in my mind God is so much more merciful to others than I think He's going to be to me.

But, if Heber C. Kimball is right, and our Father God is a cheerful pleasant, lively and good-natured Being, then wouldn't He be this way toward all His children? Wouldn't He delight to lovingly rescue any repentant child who has turned to Him for help?

The tricky part is that even when we have faith that He will rescue us, His deliverance comes in His time, not ours. So what are we to do in the meantime? Most people's first instinct is to worry, fret or even pout, barter or beg. If we can, we'll try to take control of the situation and make things happen for ourselves. Although the Lord encourages us to do what we can, if what we try doesn't work – no matter what we do – then the timing isn't right or our solution isn't the one He has in mind. It's time to step back, focus on our relationship with the Lord, serve others and wait for further directions.

Paul teaches us what kind of attitude we can have in the midst of trials: "We are troubled on every side, yet not distressed; we are perplexed, but not in despair." (2 Corinthians 4:8)

Notice we can be perplexed – we rarely know what the Lord is up to, but we do not despair because we trust Him and know He has not forsaken us.

Paul continues in 2 Corinthians 4:15-18

> "For all things are for your sakes, that the abundant grace might through the thanksgiving of many redound to the glory of God. For which cause we faint not; but though our outward man perish, yet the inward man is renewed day by day.

> "For our light affliction, which is but for a moment, worketh for us a far more exceeding and eternal weight of glory; While we look not at the things which are seen, but at the things which are not seen: for the things which are seen are temporal; but the things which are not seen are eternal."

In other words, the "affliction" we may have to suffer is "but for a moment" in the grand scheme of things and serves several purposes:

1. It serves our good (is for our sakes).
2. Sets an example and glorifies God.
3. Helps our spirit to grow stronger day by day.

4. Works for us "a far more exceeding and eternal weight of glory" (i.e. eternal rewards).

The key to being able to endure this "light affliction" (anything is light in comparison with what the Savior endured for us), is to not put too much stock in things we see with our own eyes – which are earthly and temporary. We may not be able to see the solution to our challenge. Through logical earthly eyes, all may seem lost, but if we put our trust in the Lord, He will strengthen us that our burdens become light. We can be "troubled on every side, yet not distressed… perplexed, but not in despair." (2 Corinthians 4:8) It's a matter of faith in things we cannot see.

I like Edward Teller's definition of faith, "When you get to the end of all the light you know and it's time to step into the darkness of the unknown, faith is knowing that one of two things shall happen: either you will be given something solid to stand on, or you will be taught how to fly."

As we do all we can do, step forward in faith and trust a cheerful and loving God's grace to make up the difference, He will deliver us in His perfect time. As Spencer W. Kimball said, "The problems of the world cannot possibly be solved by skeptics or cynics whose horizons are limited by the obvious realities. We need men (and women) who can dream of things that never were and ask, Why not? … We do not worry about HOW and WHEN and WHY. We say WHY NOT?"

Come Follow Me

What did Christ mean when he said, "Come follow me?" For the ancient disciples, he may have meant to literally follow Him around the countryside, but He meant more than that. He meant follow in His footsteps — do what He did, follow His actions, follow His example. But does this apply to us today? Is following Him still relevant in a modern world?

After all, our civilization is totally different than the one in which those early disciples lived. We live in a world where a letter or a picture can be sent from New York to Japan in a matter of seconds. People from every corner of the world can converse with each other with a phone call. We have television, satellites, computers, airplanes, and modern cures for diseases that would have killed our ancestors.

Common everyday occurrences for us would be miracles to Christ's early followers. Does the world still need such an ancient message — one over 2000 years old? Or have we evolved beyond the need for His message?

To decide that, we first need to know what his message was. Perhaps the greatest synopsis of Christ's message can be found in two verses:

"A new commandment I give unto you, That ye love one another; as I have loved you, that ye also love one another. By this shall all men know that ye are my disciples, if ye have love one to another." John 13:34-35

Love was His message. Love is why He died for us. Love is why he rose again that we might live. So let's see if love is still the answer to modern-day problems:

·   If we loved each other, would there be murder in the world?
·   If we loved each other, would we steal from others?
·   If we loved each other, would 50% of all marriages end in divorce?
·   If we loved each other, would wars rage?
·   If we loved each other and truly understood what love is, would there be teenage pregnancy?
·   If we loved ourselves, would there be drug and alcohol abuse?
·   If we loved Him, would we keep his commandments? (John 14:15)

Almost every modern problem could be solved with love — true love — the pure love of Christ — not lust or misdirected obsession - but pure love that is understanding, kind and longsuffering. No, His message is not ancient or out dated. It is timeless.

The Litmus Test

With so many philosophies being presented in today's world, it is easy for some to become confused or led astray. Jesus foretold that in the last days "false christs and false prophets shall rise, and shall shew signs and wonders, to seduce, if it were possible, even the elect" (Mark 13:22). So how do we determine what is false and what is true? How do we avoid being deceived? In 1 John 4, John gives us the litmus test for determining

a) how to tell if something is from God
b) how to tell if someone is truly converted to Christ.

Is It from God?

John begins the chapter with a similar warning to what Jesus gave: "Beloved, believe not every spirit, but try the spirits whether they are of God: because many false prophets are gone out into the world." He continues in verse 2 by explaining how to test or try these individuals and philosophies:

"Hereby know ye the Spirit of God: Every spirit that confesseth that Jesus Christ is come in the flesh is of God; and every spirit that confesseth not that Jesus Christ is come in the flesh is not of God: and this is that spirit of antichrist, whereof ye have heard that it should come; and even now already is it in the world" (1 John 4:2-3).

So, if something or someone teaches that Jesus is the Christ, the Messiah, and that He came in the flesh, then it is of the Spirit of God. If it denies that Jesus is the Christ, if it denies that He condescended from the heavens and came in the flesh, then it is not of God. It is the spirit of antichrist – or against Christ.

1 Thessalonians 5:21 also tells us to "prove all things; hold fast that which is good." Those things that persuade and invite us to believe in Christ and to do good are from God; whereas those things that deny Christ or persuade us to do evil are of Satan. Satan continually fights against the Lord. Satan never invites us to do good or to believe in Jesus Christ, for if he did, he would be doing as Jesus reasoned: "Every kingdom divided against itself is brought to desolation; and every city or house divided against itself shall not stand: and if Satan cast out Satan, he is divided against himself; how shall then his kingdom stand?" (Matthew 12:25-26).

Are We Truly Converted?

1 John 4:6-8 continues to explain how we can know if we, or anyone else for that matter, have the Spirit of God:

"We are of God: he that knoweth God heareth us (speaking of the apostles/ prophets); he that is not of God heareth not us. Hereby know we the spirit of truth, and the spirit of error. Beloved, let us love one another: for love is of God; and every one that loveth is born of God, and knoweth God. He that loveth not knoweth not God; for God is love."

He also says in 1 John 3:18, "My little children, let us not love in word, neither in tongue; but in deed and in truth." A true test of our conversion to Jesus Christ is found in how we treat each other – not just other believers, but everyone. Do we honestly and truly love others? Do we show that love in our actions and not just in our words?

If we love one another, God's Spirit dwells in us, and His love is perfected in us. In this way we may know whether His Spirit is in us by how we treat each other. (1 John 4:12-13)

So, by using these two tests given by John, we can avoid being deceived. We can avoid being like those of which Isaiah warned, "Woe unto them that call evil good, and good evil; that put darkness for light, and light for darkness; that put bitter for sweet, and sweet for bitter" (Isaiah 5:20). When faced with any philosophy or idea, let us ask if it persuades to believe that Jesus is the Christ and to do good. And we also may know if someone is truly converted by the love they show to others. "By their fruits ye shall know them" (Matthew 7:20).

Help Thou Mine Unbelief

In Matthew chapter 9, a man brought his deaf and dumb son to Jesus' disciples, but they could not heal him. Jesus came and found the scribes questioning his disciples and asked, "What question ye with them?" Then the man who had brought his son answered, "Master, I have brought unto thee my son, which hath a dumb spirit; and wheresoever he taketh him he teareth him: and he foameth, and gnasheth with his teeth, and pineth away: and I spake to thy disciples that they should cast him out; and they could not" (Mark 9:16-18).

Then Jesus answered him and said, "O faithless generation, how long shall I be with you? How long shall I suffer you? Bring him unto me" (Mark 9:19).

And they brought the child and immediately the spirit tore at him and he fell on the ground, and wallowed foaming. Jesus asked the father, "How long is it ago since this came unto him?" And the man answered that he had been this way since childhood, and that many times it had cast him into the fire or into the water to destroy him. Then the father pleaded, "But if thou canst do anything, have compassion on us, and help us" (Mark 9:20-22).

Think of this man's situation and perspective on his son's problem. His son had been this way since he was a little child, he'd asked the disciples for help, but they could do nothing. So here he is coming to Jesus requesting help. Everything seems to be stacked against the man and his son. Nothing seems to be working for them, but he's still willing to keep asking.

Jesus answers him, "If thou canst believe, all things are possible to him that believeth."

And straightway the father of the child cried out and said with tears, "Lord, I believe!"

Then as if to answer a questioning look from Jesus eyes, he added, "Help thou mine unbelief."

Jesus charged the deaf and dumb spirit to "come out of him and enter no more into him. The spirit cried, rent him sore, and came out of him; and he was as one dead; insomuch that many said, He is dead. But Jesus took him by the hand, and lifted him up; and he arose" (Mark 9:25-27).

Sometimes we face trials and challenges that seem insurmountable. There may appear to be no logical solution or no earthly way of healing the situation. But just as Jesus told the father in this story, "If thou canst believe, all things are possible to him that believeth."

Recently this story has taken on new meaning for me as I've grappled with a dilemma where everything seemed to be pointing me in a certain direction, but means of going in that direction were blocked. I felt the Lord was opening doors that took money and means that I didn't have available to walk through. I knew I needed to have faith and believe that He would provide the means necessary, but I still felt like this

father, "Lord I believe, help thou mine unbelief!" Like the
father, my heart was saying one thing while my circumstances screamed, "but how?"

As a matter of fact, this father's words have been running
through my mind for a solid week. Finally, the other day, I
took the opportunity to look up this passage in the Bible and
continued to read further.

Later, Jesus' disciples asked him privately why they couldn't
cast out the spirit. Jesus answered, "This kind can come forth
by nothing, but by prayer and fasting" (Mark 9:28-29).

I determined that prayer and fasting were what I needed to
cast out my spirit of doubt. But what was I supposed to fast
for? An increase in faith? The money to fund the project?
What?

While talking with a friend, she asked me if I had ever prayed
and gotten a solid answer that the doors that were opening
were really the ones God intended for me to enter. While it
seemed apparent that they were, I had never really asked. I
didn't know beyond any doubt that God intended for me to
act on these opportunities. I didn't have a solid confirmation –
hence the doubt and trepidation. She suggested that I get a
solid answer about whether this was definitely something
that I was supposed to do. If it was, then I would be able to
have the faith necessary to move forward and trust that the
Lord would provide the means in His time.

I knew she was right. Not having a definite confirmation is what had been causing my vacillation between faith and nagging doubts. So I began the fast, came to the Lord several times throughout a 24-hour period asking if my choice was the correct one. I studied the scriptures that I felt led to read, even made a pros and cons list and finally that overwhelming answer came. A feeling of peace, joy and warmth that told me the Lord was saying, "Yes, I opened these doors for you. Doubt not, fear not, walk forward and I will provide."

I have a strong testimony of the principle of prayer and fasting as outlined in Isaiah 58. As we fast, Isaiah 58:9 says, "Then shalt thou call, and the Lord shall answer; thou shalt cry, and He shall say, *Here I am.*" I testify to you that *He is there!* Our Heavenly Father listens to the prayers of every single honest seeking soul and He is ready and willing to answer the perplexing problems with which we grapple. I am grateful that the Lord looks out for each one of us, and holds out blessings that if we but have the faith, casting fear out of our hearts, we may receive. I leave these thoughts with you in the name of our Lord and Savior Jesus Christ, Amen.

Seedtime and Harvest

While visiting with my great aunt who is in her late 80's, our conversation turned to gardening. For years she was an avid gardener and as children my brother and I spent weeks at a time with her in the summers. She and her husband let us "help" them garden. As we reminisced she pointed out that each time we came, she had to teach us the difference between the plants and the weeds, and that sometimes we were really more work than we were worth because of the time it took to teach us. I can relate to this as I plant my own gardens. My little one seems to have a homing device in the soles of his shoes that leads him straight on top of the plants.

My aunt seemed to be transported back in time to those days when she would arise early and weed her garden in the cool of the morning with the chirping birds as her companions until about 10 a.m. when the sweat bees made their first appearance. She spoke of the peace and tranquility of working with her hands in "Mother Earth" and that it seemed as near to heaven on earth as she would ever get in this life. She told of how much she loved to plant and to weed her garden, and that her husband enjoyed plowing and harvest. Together they made a perfect pair of gardeners.

As she reminisced, I contrasted myself to her. I enjoy the planting and the harvest, but the weeding in between is the part I do not enjoy. Why do I hate weeding? I told her it was because I don't like bending over, but she replied that she just sat leisurely on a stool and enjoyed the morning. "I could get a stool. That would be easy enough," I thought to myself as she painted this peaceful picture of the birds chirping and the dew on the ground as she enjoyed each morning in her garden. But the more I thought about it, the more I realized that the reason I don't enjoy weeding is because I'm not consistently out there in my garden weeding it. I let it go for a week, and return to find thorny weeds taking over. It's so overwhelming by then. Sometimes I get so overwhelmed that I resign myself to only enjoying whatever harvest is hardy enough to rise above the thorny weeds. I miss out on so much because I get distracted with other things and am not consistent in weeding the garden.

My lack of consistency in weeding spills over into most other aspects of my life. I'm not a consistent being. I enjoy change and variety, but I'm also not very disciplined on anything that I don't want to be disciplined about. Yet, the older I get, the more I begin to comprehend the importance of consistency if we expect to ever reap a more-than-meager harvest. Whether it's in parenting or business or our spiritual growth, consistency is critical.

Consistently teaching and training our children and setting a diligent example for them to follow is our only hope for shielding them from the onslaughts of this world. Consistently working, marketing and learning are critical for success in any business endeavor. And consistently praying, studying, and sharing the gospel is the only way to reap spiritual rewards.

If the history of the Earth were one big growing season, where would we be? Jesus said we are in the harvest. John 4:35-38 says,

"Say not ye, There are yet four months, and then cometh harvest? Behold, I say unto you, Lift up your eyes, and look on the fields; for they are white already to harvest. And he that reapeth receiveth wages, and gathereth fruit unto life eternal: that both he that soweth and he that reapeth may rejoice together. And herein is that saying true, One soweth, and another reapeth. I sent you to reap that whereon ye bestowed no labour: other men laboured, and ye are entered into their labours."

In the history of the world, we are in the harvest. The earth is ripe, ready to be harvested. This is even truer today than it was in Jesus' time. We live in a time when the world is a spiritual vacuum. With the secularization of schools and public places and events, there are children who grow up in this world never knowing about God or spiritual things. These people are spiritually starved. There is "a famine in the land, not a famine of bread, nor a thirst for water, but of hearing the words of the Lord" (Amos 8:11). The field is most certainly white and ready to harvest on a global scale.

But, individually speaking, the people we meet are at different points in their spiritual growing season. Some need seeds planted. Others need weeding, and still others are peek and ready for harvest. Patience and consistency is such a critical part of sharing the gospel with others. We cannot expect someone to be ready for harvest when no spiritual seeds have been planted in their life. Nor can we expect them to thrive when they are still being "choked by the thorny cares of the world" (see Matthew 13:22). Just as in gardening I enjoy planting and harvest, so also I enjoy planting gospel seeds and watching them grow and look forward to a time of harvest when those individuals are ready to commit and live what they have learned.

It's the in between part that is hard – helping them weed out old habits, watching them struggle as they try to find ways to change worldly lifestyles, seeing them progress three steps and fall back two. Just as we need more laborers for harvest, I believe we need more laborers for weeding. We need more people willing to stand by their friends and family members who are struggling to overcome the choking thorns that surround them. We need more people willing to take a stand and be a good example without a "holier than thou" attitude. We need more love, patience and tolerance of those who are struggling to rise above the weeds in which they've been planted.

It takes time, love and a lot of encouragement. But most of all, it takes an eye of faith to see the potential harvest within those around us. It takes discernment to recognize the difference between plants and weeds. We must catch the vision ourselves before we can help others see the potential of who they can become. Those surrounded by weeds tend to feel that they are nothing more than weeds themselves. They often do not see that within them lies a beautiful plant with the potential for bountiful and tasty fruit. When we look at them through the eyes of our Savior, we see it. We feel and know of their potential, but they have to come to catch a vision of who they are as a child of God for themselves. It takes time for them to truly see themselves as God sees them… with all their potential for greatness. Laborers involved in that tedious time between planting and harvest must be consistently there for others to lean on. We must be their eyes — continually encouraging and reflecting a hopeful picture of what they can

become — until they've removed enough of the weeds sur-
rounding them to understand that they are something different, something precious worth saving, growing, and bearing
fruit.

Let us have faith in the harvest – not only that it will come but
also that it will come in abundance when we faithfully,
consistently, diligently and with patience keep an eye of faith
that sees others through our Savior's eyes.

Enduring in Faith

While Jesus was on his way to raise a ruler's daughter from the dead, a woman, who was diseased with an issue of blood for twelve years, came behind him and touched the hem of his garment. She had said to herself, "If I could just touch his garment, I shall be made whole." When she touched his clothing, Jesus turned around and said to her, "Daughter, be of good comfort; thy faith hath made thee whole." And she was healed that very hour. (Matthew 9:20-22)

When we read this story, we marvel at the faith that this woman had – to only touch Jesus' garment and be healed. We often marvel at Jesus himself who was so sensitive that he could tell when a portion of his power was being used by another's faith. But something we rarely think about is the life of this woman. She had spent the last twelve years hemorrhaging. And not only would this have been a total aggravation and weakened her into a state of anemia, but also she would have been an outcast from society.

We learn in Leviticus 15:19-28 that the Law of Moses required a woman with an issue of blood to be separated. Everything she touched or sat on was considered unclean. Anyone she touched or touched her was considered unclean. Even when a woman's "issue of blood" ceased, she would have been considered unclean for 7 more days and then on the 8th day she was to go and make an offering to the priests. This poor woman had been considered unclean and separated from others for twelve years! Everyone and everything she came in contact with would have been considered unclean.

Can you imagine the heartache and the pain this woman must have experienced for twelve long years? Can you imagine the prayers and the pleading and the cries she must have raised to her Father in Heaven for healing and comfort? For twelve long years no answer came. No healing occurred. Yet she never lost her faith. If anything her faith appears to have increased with her trial for she knew that all she had to do was touch Jesus' garment and she would be healed.

Did Jesus shun her as unclean? The Law of Moses would have required him to. But he did not. Instead he recognized her great faith, had compassion on her and healed her according to her faith.

Many times in our lives we must suffer for extended lengths of time – pleading for answers, for relief, for healing. Yet the answer appears to be "No." This does not mean that God does not hear our cries or that He loves us any less. It simply isn't the right time yet. Perhaps we haven't learned all we needed to learn yet. Perhaps our faith has not been molded and shaped to the extent that God knows it should be.

In three short verses, this woman sets a powerful example of enduring in faithfulness through trials that seem to go on and on. She teaches us, that we should never blame God or give up hope. Her story is one of hope – that Jesus loves us and that eventually, in God's time, through our faith (whether in this life or the next) we will be healed and the light will come.

The Spirit is Willing
But the Flesh is Weak

[Follow along with this lesson in Matthew 26,
Mark 14, Luke 22, and John 18.]

At the feast of the Passover, Jesus sat down with his disciples
in a large upper room of a building (Luke 22:12). It was there
that Christ instituted the sacrament or Lord's supper. He took
the bread, gave thanks, broke it and gave it to them saying,
"This is my body which is given for you: this do in remembrance of me." Then he took the cup and said, "This cup is the
new testament in my blood, which is shed for you" (Luke
22:19).

Christ foretold of his own death and resurrection. Whenever
we partake of this ordinance we do so in "remembrance" of
him. We remember his body that he gave and the blood that he
shed for us. The symbols of this ordinance are designed to
remind us of his sacrifice and our devotion. God knows that it
is human nature to forget. We can be zealous one day and
forgetful the next. This fact is evident in the events that
followed the Lord's supper.

After Judas had left to betray him, Jesus prophesied to his
disciples that even they would scatter and deny him. Peter
insisted that "Although all shall be offended, yet will not I."
But Jesus said to him, "Verily I say unto thee, That this day,
even in this night, before the cock crow twice, thou shalt deny
me thrice." In shock, Peter spoke vehemently, "If I should die

with thee, I will not deny thee in any wise." The rest of the disciples agreed. (Mark 14:29-31)

After this, Jesus took his disciples to the garden of Gethsemane. He asked his disciples to "Sit ye here, while I shall pray." Then, he took Peter, James and John and began to be sorrowful and very heavy. (Matthew 26:37) Mark 14:33 tells us that he "began to be sore amazed, and to be very heavy." What torment, what anguish would cause the very Son of God to be amazed? He asked them to "Pray that ye enter not into temptation" (Luke 22:40). and then withdrew himself "about a stone's cast, and kneeled down and prayed, saying 'Father, if thou be willing, remove this cup from me: nevertheless not my will, but thine, be done.' And there appeared an angel unto him from heaven, strengthening him. And being in an agony he prayed more earnestly: and his sweat was as it were great drops of blood falling down to the ground" (Luke 22:41-44).

What torment, what anguish he must have suffered as the weight of our sins began to descend upon him in the garden! So great was his pain that his Father sent an angel to strengthen him. Yet where were his disciples? They were only a stone's cast away, yet when he rose from his prayer and went over to them he found them sleeping. He said to them, "What, could ye not watch with me one hour? Watch and pray, that ye enter not into temptation: the spirit indeed is willing, but the flesh is weak" (Matthew 26:40-42).

His disciples seemed almost oblivious to the importance of the events that were occurring at that moment. Where were they when He needed them to stand by him and support him in his darkest hour? They were asleep. How many of us fall asleep spiritually when he needs us? Do we slumber in apathy in a world filled with evil? Never waking up to be a part of the solution? Or do we stand up and be counted, giving support and encouragement to those on the side of truth and righteousness? Even an encouraging word can do much to alleviate the burdens of those around us. Even one word in defense of truth may be enough to make others who are too timid to stand up for what is right come forth in boldness.

As he was speaking to them, a large group of people came, led by Judas who betrayed him with a kiss. John tells us that Peter drew his sword and cut off the ear of the high priest's servant. Jesus told him to "Put up again thy sword into his place for all they that take the sword shall perish with the sword" (Matthew 26:52). Then Jesus immediately reached forth his hand and healed the servant. (Luke 22:51) Jesus wanted his disciples to be there for him, stand up and be counted, but not through violence. Fighting with the sword was not the answer here.

Christ was then taken, bound and carried before chief priests and elders. Just as Christ had prophesied, the sheep scattered when their shepherd was taken. (Matthew 26:31) Each of the disciples ran off. But Peter followed from a distance that he might learn what would become of his Lord. He followed him into the high priest's palace and sat with the servants to see what would happen (Matthew 26:58). One by one, false witnesses who contradicted each other came forth. Most likely they were paid for their testimony. "But Jesus held his peace." Matthew 26:63.

What composure, what a knowledge of his mission He had! How many of us could stand still, never saying a word while we were falsely accused? Yet, Jesus knew this was what his Father wanted. He knew that the salvation of souls hung in the balance and that he must submit to these preposterous allegations. How many of us cannot even withstand the ridicule and taunting words of seeming friends or family who would not physically harm us, much less stand before enemies who seek our death?

As Christ was questioned, Peter sat down to warm himself next to a group of people who were huddled by a fire that was kindled in the midst of the hall. A maid saw him, looked at him earnestly — as if to study his face and said, " This man was also with him." But Peter denied it and said, "Woman I know him not." A little while passed and another person saw him and said, "Thou art also of them." But Peter answered with an oath, "Man, I am not" (Luke 22:55-58, Matthew 26:72).

A third time, someone came up to Peter and said, "Surely thou also art one of them; for thy speech betrayeth thee." Then Peter began to curse and to swear saying, "I know not the man." And immediately the cock crew. Peter then remembered the word of Jesus which said unto him, Before the cock crow, thou shalt deny me thrice. And he went out and wept bitterly" (Matthew 26:73-75).

Before the cock crew and before Peter realized what he had done, he just wanted to fit in with the crowd. He didn't want to stand out as someone associated with Jesus Christ. If it meant swearing and cursing to prove he was not associated, to prove he fit in with the rest, then so be it. Fear of men overtook him at that point. Not until the cock crew did he realize what he had done and shrank off in remorse. What do we do in our own lives just to fit in? Just to be popular? Just so we don't rock the boat? Do we realize the price we pay for our cowardice? Do we realize that we are denying our Lord when we shrink from living as an example of Him to others?

Just a few hours earlier Peter had promised that he would never deny him. That very evening he had joined in the Lord's supper and ate the bread and drank the wine in remembrance of Him. He had even been so bold as to draw his sword in Christ's defense in the garden, yet by morning he had forgotten Christ's words and denied him three times. How soon we forget! How soon we slacken our faith and lose our confidence in the Lord. No wonder we must be continually reminded to remember him.

But in Peter we find hope for even the weakest of us — even for those of us who are scared to stand up for the Savior in front of our friends and family. Peter later became a great prophet who led the Church after Christ's resurrection and ascension. Peter grew in his spiritual strength. Over time, he became as strong as one could be in standing up for the Savior. So there is hope for us. If we will look to Christ, pray continually that we may resist temptation, remember him, learn of him and practice standing up for Him, one day we will be strong in the face of opposition. We will be able to say to anyone who asks, "For I am not ashamed of the gospel of Christ: for it is the power of God unto salvation to every one that believeth" (Romans 1:16).

My God, My God, Why Hast Thou Forsaken Me?

Thick darkness covered the land of Jerusalem while Jesus hung on the cross. And about the ninth hour Jesus cried with a loud voice, saying, "Eli, Eli, lama sabchtani?" That is to say, "My God, my God, why hast thou forsaken me?" (Matthew 27:46) Why did Jesus feel that his God, His Father, had forsaken him?

First, the Father cannot look upon sin with the least degree of allowance and here Jesus was — carrying the weight and sins of the world on his shoulders. All our mistakes, iniquities and infirmities were upon him as he hung on the cross. His Father had to let him go through this alone. Perhaps even the Father could not bear to watch what they had done to his perfect, innocent Son.

But, I believe there is a second reason that Jesus chose to say the words, "My God, my God, why hast thou forsaken me?" These same words begin the 22nd Psalm. The Jews of the time knew the scriptures. Those religious leaders who had him crucified, new the scriptures so well that they could quote them verbatim. Imagine if someone came to a minister today and started the 23rd Psalm, "The Lord is my shepherd, I shall not want..." Don't you think a minister could finish that psalm? Of course. Well, the Jewish leaders of Christ's time could finish any of those psalms as easily as we could the 23rd.

The 22nd Psalm is a foreshadowing, a prophecy of Jesus Christ's atonement. In this lesson, we will compare the 22nd Psalm with the fulfillment of this prophecy found in the four gospels.

Psalms 22

1 "My God, my God, why hast thou forsaken me? Why art thou so far from helping me, and from the words of my roaring?"

This is the verse that Jesus started on the cross, hoping that the religious leaders of his time would awake to what they had done and repent.

6 But I am a worm, and no man; a reproach of men, and despised of the people.

Was Jesus not despised and reproached of men? Matthew 27:29-30 tells us that "And when they had platted a crown of thorns, they put it upon his head, and a reed in his right hand; and they bowed the knee before him, and mocked him, saying, Hail, King of the Jews! And they spit upon him and took the reed and smote him on the head."

7-8 All they that see me laugh me to scorn: they shoot out the lip, they shake the head saying, He trusted on the LORD that he would deliver him: let him deliver him, seeing he delighted in him.

Compare Matthew 27:39-43: "And they that passed by reviled him, wagging their heads, and saying, Thou that destroyest the temple, and buildest it in three days, save thyself. If thou be the Son of God, come down from the cross. Likewise also the chief priests mocking him, with the scribes and elders said, He saved others; himself he cannot save. If he be the King of Israel, let him now come down from the cross, and we will believe him."

9-10 But thou art he that took me out of the womb: thou didst make me hope when I was upon my mother's breasts. I was cast upon thee from the womb: thou art my God from my mother's belly.

As the angel Gabriel told Mary, "Fear not, Mary for thou hast found favor with God. And behold thou shalt conceive in thy womb, and bring forth a son, and shalt call his name Jesus. He shall be great, and shall be called the Son of the Highest; and the Lord God shall give unto him the throne of his father David... The Holy Ghost shall come upon thee, and the power of the Highest shall overshadow thee; therefore also that holy thing which shall be born of thee shall be called the Son of God" (Luke 1:30-32,35).

14,16 I am poured out like water, and all my bones are out of joint: my heart is like wax; it is melted in the midst of my bowels. For dogs have compassed me: the assembly of the wicked have enclosed me: they pierced my hands and my feet.

Does this not describe the pain and agony of the cross? John 19:32 - 34 explains, "Then came the soldiers, and brake the legs of the first, and of the other which was crucified with him. But when they came to Jesus, and saw that he was dead already, they brake not his legs: But one of the soldiers with a spear pierced his side, and forthwith came there out blood and water." Modern doctors have said that the only way that blood and water could have poured out would be if Jesus had died of a massive heart failure. Jesus died of a broken heart.

15 My strength is dried up like a potsherd; and my tongue cleaveth to my jaws; and thou hast brought me into the dust of death.

"After this, Jesus knowing that all things were now accomplished, that the scripture might be fulfilled, saith, I thirst. Now there was set a vessel full of vinegar: and they filled a sponge with vinegar, and put it upon hyssop, and put it to his mouth." John 19:28-29

18 They part my garments among them, and cast lots upon my vesture.

Compare John 19:23 - 24, "Then the soldiers, when they had crucified Jesus, took his garments, and made four parts, to every soldier a part; and also his coat: now the coat was without seam, woven from the top throughout."

"They said therefore among themselves, Let us not rend it, but cast lots for it, whose it shall be: that the scripture might be fulfilled, which saith, They parted my raiment among them, and for my vesture they did cast lots. These things therefore the soldiers did."

So, as Jesus spoke, "My God, my God, why hast thou forsaken me," surely those who crucified him, could not help but finish Psalm 22 and know what they had done to their Lord, even the very Son of God.

Beyond Reach?

Someone once wrote me for advice. Her preacher stated that a person could get so far away from God that He is unable to help or reach them. My immediate reaction was that the preacher's statement is completely preposterous. Is anything too difficult for the Lord? I think not!

In particular a quote by Virginia U. Jenson came to mind: "His knowledge of you goes beyond a catalog of your deeds. He knows you individually and completely. He understands your darkest hours when things seem as black as a cave with no light. He understands when you are feeling unworthy or forgotten or depressed or desperate or alone. He constantly and gently invites you to open up those dark recesses of your heart to Him that He may fill them with His light. You can't shock Him. You can't surprise Him. He won't turn away from you in disgust, shaking His head and saying, 'Oh, this is worse than I thought. There's nothing I can do here.' When He healed the sick, He often forgave their sins as well. His healing extends to the crippled heart just as surely as to the crippled leg." [1]

Clearly with God, nothing is impossible! (Luke 1:37) Then there's Isaiah's comforting logic, "Come now, and let us reason together, saith the LORD: though your sins be as scarlet, they shall be as white as snow; though they be red like crimson, they shall be as wool" (Isaiah 1:18).

So why would this preacher say that someone could get too far away from God to be reachable? I wondered if I could be missing something. As I pondered on the matter, I found Isaiah chapter 59. In this chapter Isaiah talks about how Israel is separated from their God by iniquity. He says, "Behold the Lord's hand is not shortened, that it cannot save; neither his ear heavy, that it cannot hear."

But in the very next sentence and thereafter Isaiah warns, "But your iniquities have separated between you and your God, and your sins have hid his face from you, that He will not hear. For your hands are defiled with blood, and your fingers with iniquity; your lips have spoken lies, your tongue hath muttered perverseness." He continues to expound upon their iniquities throughout the chapter. This sounds a lot like the preacher's statement, does it not? It sounds like these people are beyond reach and that God is closed off to their cries.

Is this true then? Can someone really go so far that God will no longer hear or help them? It is my opinion that this is only true for as long as the person allows it to be true. It is a choice on the individual's part. In essence, this individual has refused God's help and chosen a different master. It isn't that God has shortened His hand that it cannot save. It is not that His ear is deaf. It is that the individual has allowed sin and iniquity to clog the channels of communication between him and the Lord. The sinner's ear is deaf and will not follow the Master. For how can a person know a Master whom he has not served or who is a stranger to him and is far from the thoughts and intents of his heart? As Jesus said, "my sheep hear my voice, and I know them and they follow me" (John 10:27).

But the moment that individual repents of his or her sins and turns to God, spiritual eyes are opened and spiritual ears can hear. Isaiah assures us at the end of chapter 59 that "the

Redeemer will come to those who will turn from their trans-
gression."

Just because a person is not able to hear or see today, doesn't
mean that that same individual will not be receptive to the
voice of the Shepherd a month, a year or 20 years from now.
God has a way of leading people "line upon line, precept
upon precept, here a little, there a little" (Isaiah 28:10-13) until
their ears hear, their eyes open, their hearts understand, and
they are converted so Christ may heal them (see Matthew
13:15).

The bottom line of the matter is that God will never force the
human heart. He will gently persuade, lead and guide. He
will chasten those He loves – which is every last one of us - in
hopes that we will be humble enough to repent and turn to
Him (Hebrews 12:6). But there is no one who has gone so far
that God will refuse His redeeming hand should they turn to
Him. No repentant seeker is beyond His reach or His healing
touch. He says to all, "Every one that thirsteth, come ye to the
waters, and he that hath no money; come ye, buy, and eat; yea,
come, buy wine and milk without money and without price.
Incline your ear, and come unto me: hear, and your soul shall
live; and I will make an everlasting covenant with you"
(Isaiah 55:1,3).

Don't let anyone ever tell you that you or someone you love
has gone too far or that there is no hope. Through Christ there
is *always* hope! No one is beyond reach.

1) Virginia U. Jensen, *I Can Do All Things Through Christ*, The
Best of Women's Conference, Bookcraft 2000, p. 234

I Can Do All Things Through Christ

As I ponder on the Life of Jesus Christ, His love for us and His mission, I am reminded of His characteristics and attributes which I would like to emulate in my own life.

One of the qualities I love best about my Savior is His meekness and humility in complete obedience. He was taken as a lamb to the slaughter and submitted Himself to the will of the Father in all things, thus offering Himself a ransom for each one of us – billions upon billions of us. Jesus never doubted His power, but He also never ceased to meekly acknowledge the Source of that power. In John 8:28 he explained, "I do nothing of myself, but as my Father hath taught me." I find such strength in this single principle of knowing on Whom we can rely. Like Paul I rejoice that I can indeed "do all things through Christ which strengtheneth me" (Philippians 4:13). What a comfort it is to know that we are not alone in this world! Wickedness, war and depravity may surround us, but with God on our side, nothing is impossible. While an honest soul will acknowledge her own nothingness before Him, that same humble individual can take comfort in knowing the limitless power available to her through the Savior. We need not doubt when we put our trust in Him. When we rely on His love, light, grace and strength everything will work together for our good.

Among the items of good news that Jesus Christ brings is that we are not alone. When we face situations where we do not know how to proceed, we can be confident that if the Lord has brought us to it, He will bring us through it. Just before the agonizing hours of Gethsemane and Calvary, Jesus told his disciples, "Be of good cheer." How could He say this? There could have been no darker hours for the disciples and the world as a whole than in those in which the God of heaven suffered and the earth quaked in anguish for her Maker. How could He say, "Be of good cheer" in such circumstances? He explains, "In the world ye shall have tribulation: but be of good cheer; I have overcome the world" (John 16:33).

Those same hours which brought such anguish and heart-ache for those who loved Him made it possible for those who would ever love Him to obtain a remission of their sins, rise in the resurrection and receive eternal life in the kingdom of heaven. What better reason do we have to be of good cheer than that Jesus Christ has overcome sin, death and everything else the world throws at us?

As we walk through the dark hours of our own lives, we can take comfort in knowing that just as Sunday's resurrection morning followed the bleak hours of Gethsemane and Calvary so will God's blessings follow our own miniature Gethsemanes. I testify that He is risen and He still lives and loves each one of us, and because He lives we may too. In Jesus name, Amen.

Building Your House of Faith

If you were remodeling your home and were going to add an extra bedroom, but the only tool you had was a screwdriver, would you work and struggle to build the room with only a screwdriver? Or would you go out to the store and pay the price for the proper tools to get the job done efficiently and effectively?

Many of us try to build our houses of faith with one favorite tool that we've gotten used to. We either don't realize that there are more tools available or we're not willing to pay the price to acquire them. A house of faith is built first and foremost upon an open mind. William James once said, "In admitting a new body of evidence, we instinctively seek to disturb as little as possible, our pre-existing stock of ideas." Most of us try to make new concepts, truths or ideas fit within the framework of our pre-existing conditioning. We don't ask, "Will this concept make my life better?" instead we ask, "Does this fit with what I already believe?" But, in order to gain the tools of knowledge and truth that we need to build our house of faith, we will need to ask the first question, "Will this concept or idea make my life better?" If the answer is yes, then we should seriously study and consider it. Just because something doesn't fit within our pre-existing understanding of the world, does not mean that it is wrong, invalid, or cannot dramatically improve our life.

Jesus taught that we do not put new wine into old bottles lest they burst and break. (Matthew 9:17) People who are staunchly tied to their own ideas and traditions – the old way of doing things can't handle the "new wine" or the new information that God has to share with them. They cast it away in their unbelief and never give it a chance. They don't put it to the test - plant the seed, see if it sprouts and begins to bear fruit. This is why God told us to "lean not upon thine own understanding" (Proverbs 3:5).

Recently, I've had the opportunity to learn some brand new ideas – revolutionary ideas to me that are making significant improvements in my level of faith and understanding of how God works in our lives. Sometimes the things I'm learning make me a little unsettled because they sort of clash with some pre-conceived notions. But when I ask myself, "Assuming this is true, will this information make my life better?" the answer I get is a resounding "Yes." I've started planting the seeds and they're growing and bearing good fruit. Thus, I now know that they are good seeds.

I am coming to understand that the wealth of knowledge, light and truth that God wishes to share with us is endless, but we control the amount of it we receive by our willingness or unwillingness to lay aside our preconceived notions and absorb a little more truth.

A second way we build a house of faith is by using the tools God has given us – the scriptures (the words of His prophets), prayer, attending church regularly, and leaning on each other. It is so important for us to build relationships with other believers – other people who are walking their talk and living their faith and bearing good fruit. If the important people in your life are not conducive to a house of faith, then you do not have to divorce yourself from them, but you can spend less time with them – go less and stay for a shorter period of time.

Start building relationships with people who will help you build your house of faith.

I remember as a new mother attending church each week, sitting in the mother's lounge with the women who had several children. They seemed to have an answer to all my new mother questions. All the things I fretted and worried about were "old hat" for them. They gave me a peace and a calmness with their answers and their assurances that, "yes, we all feel that way at one time or another." What a blessing these sisters were to me! They saved me so much anxiety, searching and worry. Similarly, there are people in this world, who, if you build associations with them and make them a regular part of your life, can take the mystery out of life. They can allay your fears, strengthen your knowledge and bolster your faith.

Knowing that these tools are available why would you limit yourself to the one or two tools you may have in your toolbox? Why try to build your faith with only a screwdriver when there's a whole toolbox out there? Isn't it worth the price of a few ruffled feathers or a momentary uneasiness in your preconceived notions to have the tools to build your house of faith in an efficient and effective manner? Why dawdle and waste years of time working with a limited number of tools? The price you pay may be that your house of faith never becomes all it could be or worse, never gets built at all.

The Influence of a Righteous Mother

As I look back over my life and the influence that my mother had on me, I realize that the things she taught me have never left my memory. They are burned into my character and will stay there forever. A righteous mother's influence for good spans the generations and touches the lives of so many more than her own children. Her influence radiates in the lives of her children, her grandchildren and great-grandchildren and out to all they come in contact.

There are five attributes my mother possesses that are worth modeling. Unfortunately, the apple has fallen far from the tree on some of these characteristics. I feel that I (and everyone else in the world) would do well to incorporate these five principles into their lives.

Work Hard

My mother was always working. I'm not talking about a career really, although she did have a good career before marrying my father and having children with him. She was always working. She was cleaning, cooking, planting flowers, working in the yard, or teaching us to do the same. We had regular jobs that we had to do. She taught us that being part of a family meant everyone chipped in — not just the mother slaving thanklessly while no one else lifted a finger. She got in there with us and showed us how to work, taught us the

proper way to vacuum, to dust, to mop, to wash dishes. She
instilled an intense desire to work for what we wanted in life.

Waste Not a Minute

My mother taught us to use our time wisely. We learned
quickly that you don't tell Mama that you're bored. If you did,
you'd quickly be given some household chores to enliven your
day. If we fought or quarreled, we were put to work. My
mother lived by the motto that an "idle mind is the devil's
workshop." Constructive use of time was paramount, and
that principle is indelibly burned into the character of her
children.

Keep Your Word

My oldest sister fondly refers to my mother as, "The burning
bush." If my mother said it would happen - regardless of
whether it was punishment or reward - it would be carried
out. So let it be written; so let it be done. She didn't make
promises she wasn't prepared to keep. If she promised you
something, even if something else came up to intervene, she
would still find a way to carry out her promises. In all my
years of living, I can't recall that my mother ever told a single
lie. Her character was and is beyond reproach.

Be Consistent

My mother was ever consistent. There were no surprises. If
you disobeyed, you knew you'd reap the assigned consequences. When it comes to her devotion to God, she is ever

faithful, ever true. My mother saw that we were in church ever Sunday. Only on rare occasions, in cases of definite illness, did we miss a Sunday. She taught consistency and faithfulness by example. Although one could hardly say I am consistent in raising my children, at least her consistency in her devotion to God has worked its way deep into my mind.

Serve Others

My mother has one of those sixth senses about serving other people. In the morning I can use the last of my fabric softener, and who is to turn up on my doorstep that afternoon, but my mother carrying a brand new bottle of fabric softener. The woman is amazing. She anticipates the needs and desires of her children with the intuition of a psychic. She lives to serve her children and others.

These five characteristics that my mother possesses in such intensity affects not only her own children, but also her grandchildren. And as her children and grandchildren go out and attempt to follow in her footsteps others are blessed and impacted for good. The example of a righteous mother avails much, spans the generations and permeates to all within the reach of those she touches.

A Sacrifice or an Investment?

"She was a young girl. She had sacrificed her worldly plans
to spend long, tedious hours at work in order to provide for
and raise her younger orphan brother, but now she lay on her
bed dying of a sickness. She called her bishop, and as she
talked to him in her last moments, he held her rough, hard,
work-calloused hands in his. Then she asked the question,
"How will God know that I am His?" Gently he raised her
wrist and answered, "Show Him your hands."

"Someday we will see that pair of hands that sacrificed so
much for us. Are our hands clean and do they show the signs
of being in His service? Are our hearts pure and filled with
His thoughts?"[1] Are you prepared to offer your bodily appetites and desires to serve Him? Are you willing to "present
your bodies a living sacrifice, holy acceptable unto God,
which is your reasonable service?" (Romans 12: 10)

There is an eternal law in place called *The Law of Sacrifice*. In
the Old Testament, the Israelites sacrificed the firstlings of
their flocks in burnt offerings, sin offerings and peace offerings. When they brought the animals to be sacrificed, it was a
time of rejoicing and thanksgiving to the Lord. This was a
"shadow of things to come" – the atonement of Jesus Christ.
(Hebrews 10:1) Today, we no longer offer animal sacrifices,
but we remember the Savior's sacrifice through the sacrament
of the Lord's supper that He instituted in the Upper Room.

"Without sacrifice there is no true worship of God... 'The
Father gave his Son, and the Son gave his

life,' and we do not worship unless we give — give of our substance, . . . our time, . . . strength, . . . talent, . . . faith, . . . [and] testimonies." [2] As Hebrews 13: 16 says, "But to do good and to communicate forget not: for with such sacrifices God is well pleased."

The Law of Sacrifice could also be called the Law of Happiness, for those who understand and live the Law of Sacrifice quickly learn that sacrificing to serve the Lord is really no sacrifice at all. As the Master said, "If any man will come after me, let him deny himself, and take up my cross, and follow me. For whosoever will save his life shall lose it: and whosoever will lose his life for my sake shall find it" (Matthew 16:24-25).

"It is not a sacrifice to live the gospel of Jesus Christ. It is never a sacrifice when you get back more than you give. It is an investment, . . . a greater investment than any. . . . Its dividends are eternal and everlasting." [3]

1) Ezra Taft Benson, "Jesus Christ – Gifts and Expectations," Christmas Devotional, 7 Dec. 1986
2) *Teachings of Gordon B. Hinckley* [1997], 565.
3) *Teachings of Gordon B. Hinckley*, 567–68.

God Is Not Limited
By Appearances

How many times have you needed or wanted something in your life, but you looked around at things as they were and thought, "That's impossible. There's just no way." Perhaps you've had repeated setbacks or you're looking at your life and seeing disease, betrayal, financial distress, a broken marriage, an unbelieving spouse or whatever challenge you're facing and for all practical appearances there seems to be no way out.

In 1 Samuel, the Lord sent Samuel to select the next king from among the sons of Jesse. A strong strapping young man was brought forward and in Samuel's mind, he looked like the best prospect. But the Lord told Samuel, "Look not on his countenance, or on the height of his stature; because I have refused him: for the Lord seeth not as man seeth; for man looketh on the outward appearance, but the Lord looketh on the heart" (1 Samuel 16:7).

In essence, the Lord was telling Samuel, "Things are not as they appear. Start looking at people and things the way I do, and you'll see something truly amazing." In this instance, the Lord saw the youngest son, a small lad named David who would later become a great king of Israel.

The Lord doesn't look on appearances. The current "results" that are out there in our lives are not necessarily the truth. What is in our hearts is the truth. Proverbs 23:7 tells us, "For as [a man or woman] thinketh in his/her heart, so is s/he."

What is in our hearts determines our realities. Someone once said that a thought reaps an act, an act reaps a habit, a habit reaps a character and a character reaps a destiny. The seeds of thought we sow today, determine our ultimate destiny.

In Paul's excellent lecture on faith found in Hebrews 11 he lists a myriad of individuals who lived by faith then says that they had the ability to see the promises from "afar off" (Hebrews 11:13). They saw promises that not only they would receive, but also that we as their posterity would receive.

In the famous verse found in Hebrews 11:1 Paul explains, "Now faith is the substance of things hoped for, the evidence of things not seen." We usually stop right there, but if we continue reading, in verse 3 he says, "Through faith we understand that the worlds were framed by the word of God, so that things which are seen were not made of things which do appear."

God is not limited by appearances, circumstances or present results. He doesn't need to create your blessings or solutions out of what's currently happening in your life. Faith is the substance from which He creates your miracle. Can you see faith? Can you touch it? Does it appear before you in physical form? No! Faith is that "which does not appear," but from which God creates results in physical, tangible form in your life.

The skeptic may say, "Well, that's just impossible. How can you create something physical from that which you cannot see?" Jesus answered this question plainly, "With men this is impossible, but with God all things are possible" (Matthew

19:26). But what kind of faith is required here? Is it simply to believe that God is? Is it to believe that Jesus is the Christ? That's part of it, but there's more. Hebrews 11:6 explains the two parts to an active, miracle-producing faith:

"But without faith it is impossible to please Him: for he that cometh to God **must believe that He is, and that He is a rewarder of them that diligently seek Him.**"

So if we want to please God, we have to have faith in two things:

1.   Believe that He is
2.   Believe that He rewards those who diligently seek Him

Not only do we need to believe *in* Christ, but we need to *believe Him* when He says that nothing is impossible through Him. He tell us not to look at appearances because He's not limited by them. There's nothing that is broken that He cannot mend. There is nothing so hopeless that He can not remedy it. There is no weakness that He cannot transform into a strength (Hebrews 11:34).

A third point to ponder here is that if we believe that God rewards those who diligently seek Him, then we will not be foolish enough to believe that God will reward those who do not! True faith leads to action.

Paul asked the Corinthians, "Do ye look on things after the outward appearance? If any man trust to himself that he is Christ's, let him of himself think this again, that, as he is Christ's, even so are we Christ's" (2 Corinthians 10:7).

If we are Christ's – if we are diligently seeking Him as Hebrews 11:6 says, then we don't need to look on the outward appearances of people, things or circumstances. They aren't the truth. A Christian author named Wallace D. Wattles wrote in the early 1900's, "Every man has the natural and inherent power to think what he wants to think, but it requires far more effort to do so than it does to think the thoughts which are suggested by appearances. To think according to appearance is easy; to think truth regardless of appearances is laborious, and requires the expenditure of more power than any other work man is called upon to perform."

When the Lord is telling us to have faith, He's telling us to think truth regardless of appearances, and that's not an easy task. It takes sustained mental effort to think truth – especially when appearances are screaming that the truth is a lie! I find it profound that the Savior taught "I am the way, **the truth**, and the life: no man cometh unto the Father, but by me" (John 14:6).

Are you looking for a way out? Jesus is the way. Are you straining to have faith? Start thinking truth regardless of appearances. Jesus is that Truth. Fix your eyes on the Master and trust that He can fix whatever is broken in your life. It may look totally hopeless from man's perspective. Appearances may shout that there is no point in trying anymore. But look to Jesus Christ and you see the way; you see the truth; you see life breathed back into that broken situation. Do not limit God's ability to bless you with your miracle by wallowing in appearances. Look to Christ, doubt not, fear not.

Go Forward in Faith

One of my favorite Christian speakers related a story about
her freshman year at a large university. She was an excellent
basketball player in high school and really wanted to try out
for the college team. But in 1971 this tall, talented ball player
was painfully shy. It took everything she could muster just to
pick up the phone and research where she needed to go to try
out for the team. She went to the appointed place and stood
outside the gym for three hours, debating on whether to go
inside. But fear got the best of her, and she walked away,
never to try out for the team.

Today this talented speaker is a successful businesswoman
and great orator. Somewhere along the way she conquered her
fears. Recently she was asked to come speak to the athletes at
her university alma mater. She told the young people her story
of being too timid to pursue a spot on the college basketball
team and commended them for having the courage to pursue
their dreams. After her speech concluded, an older woman
came up to her and told her, "I remember that 1971 women's
basketball team because I was their coach. We only had 9 girls
on that team. The whole year we looked for our tenth player
we needed for scrimmages but never found her." She was that
missing player! She could have walked on that team if she
had only had the courage to walk in the building and try out.

For this confident woman now 30 years later, I'm sure she
was sickened by the knowledge that she was so close to her
dream, but had missed out just because of fears that now seem
so silly. But those fears were real to her then. After hearing

this story, I couldn't help but ask myself, "When this life is over and I am able to review it through the Lord's eyes, will I see times when He could have blessed me with more abundance, opportunities, and rich experiences, but I walked away from them because of my fears?"

The children of Israel, en mass, walked away from their Promised Land because of their fears. In Deuteronomy 1, Moses reviews the history of the Israelites and why they had to spend 40 years wandering in the wilderness. When the children of Israel arrived at the Promised Land, the Lord through Moses told them, "Behold, I have set the land before you: go in and possess the land which the LORD sware unto your fathers, Abraham, Isaac, and Jacob, to give unto them and to their seed after them... Behold, the LORD thy God hath set the land before thee: go up and possess it...fear not, neither be discouraged" (Deuteronomy 1:8,21).

But the people wanted to know what they were getting themselves into. They wouldn't march forward in simple faith in what the Lord had promised. They wanted to send 12 spies into the land to check it out first. So spies were selected and 10 of them came back with a fearful report complaining about the giants that were in the land and how they couldn't beat them. But Caleb and Joshua declared that the land was good and surely the Lord would give it to them. But the people listened to the fearful report and refused to go up to the land. As a result, they were doomed to wander in the wilderness for forty years. All the adults lost their opportunity to enter the Promised Land except faithful Joshua and Caleb.

When the Lord tells us that He will give us something, do we hesitate in fear? I know I have at times. Whether it's fear of what others may think, our enemies, our own weaknesses, or fear of failure or success, all of it will seem silly when we look back on our lives years from now. We'll wonder why we threw away precious opportunities because we were afraid of something so foolish. We'll wonder why we wasted years of our lives refusing the Lord's blessings when we were **so close** - so very close.

Don't hold yourself back because you don't know the road that lies ahead. Don't send out "spies" and believe their fearful reports. Trust the Lord. Walk forward in faith on the path you know He has prepared for you. Don't worry that you might not be good enough to fight the fight or walk the path. Don't worry about those who may oppose you. It's not you that will do the fighting. Put your trust in the Lord, and He will fight your battles and make you strong enough to bear the burden. Don't throw away months, years or a lifetime of precious opportunities just because of fears that years from now will seem so frivolous and petty.

May we live our lives without regret. "Be strong and of a good courage, fear not, nor be afraid of them: for the Lord thy God, He it is that doth go with thee; He will not fail thee, nor forsake thee" (Deuteronomy 31:6). The Lord has set your Promised Land before you. Go up and possess it!

Crossroads and Mustard Seeds

Have you ever stood at a crossroads in your life where you weren't sure which way to go? Perhaps you knew which path was the right one, but it still seemed so unsure. Maybe it looked unpopular. Maybe it felt lonely. Perhaps it appeared downright impossible and scary. As you stood at this cross-roads, you wanted to do the right thing with all your heart and soul, but it was so daunting that perhaps you hesitated. You may even have backed up in reverse. The desire was there, but you didn't know "how" you could possibly travel that road with success.

When faced with crossroads in life, it's often not a question of knowing which path is the one God wants you to take as it is a matter of needing to know how God is going to help you down that path. Interestingly enough, God rarely shows us those details. Those of us who find comfort and stability in knowing how things are going to play out also have an intense need to control our environments and destinies. We find it frightening to stand at a crossroad knowing that the only way to reach our desired destination is to forge ahead into the unknown on a path that requires surrender of our need to control. "Surrendering" is not an easy prospect, but it is one that must occur in order for us to be able to take even one step down the most wonderful of all paths. Walking this path involves surrendering your will to God and trusting Him to figure out the "how" of working all things together for your good. Once you surrender, you soon learn that He always does.

Surrendering requires faith – a leap of faith. And surprisingly it really doesn't take that much of it. It only takes a particle. Jesus used the mustard seed to illustrate this point. In Matthew 17:20, He told His disciples that if they had faith as a grain of mustard seed, they could say unto a mountain, "Remove hence to yonder place; and it shall remove; and nothing shall be impossible unto you."

Why does it take just a tiny seed of faith to work the impossible? Because that tiny particle of faith is what is necessary to commit to the path that leads to complete surrender to God's will. Once we choose to commit and take steps down God's path, we begin to see that the pathway, which once looked so dark and foreboding, is now lit ahead for a footstep or two. With each step we take, the next step is lit. If we stay the course and don't panic in self-doubt and turn back, we learn to trust Him. Our faith grows, and we learn that although "with men this is impossible, with God all things are possible" (Matthew 19:26).

In Matthew 13:31-32 Jesus gave the parable of the mustard seed. "The kingdom of heaven is like to a grain of mustard seed, which a man took, and sowed in his field: Which indeed is the least of all seeds: but when it is grown, it is the greatest among herbs, and becometh a tree, so that the birds of the air come and lodge in the branches thereof."

The little kingdom that Jesus organized during his earthly ministry has grown into a mighty tree that brings shelter and comfort to an entire world. Yet, beneath the more global church-wide symbolism for the kingdom of God is the king-

dom of God that is within each of us that all starts with a tiny
little particle of faith no bigger than a mustard seed. Each of
us holds within ourselves the seeds of greatness. Each of us
has the ability within us, if we submit ourselves to God, to
grow and flourish into someone more wonderful than we ever
imagined possible.

Through faith, Jesus taught we could move mountains and
that nothing would be impossible for us. Starting with that
first leap of faith to surrender to Him, through time, experience and living in accordance with His teachings, our tiny
seed of faith grows until it becomes a great tree-sized herb.
Notice that the mustard seed grows into a tree that helps
others. Its seeds can be used in food and its branches are a
home to the birds. So too, as your faith grows it will lead you
to become a mighty instrument in His hands to selflessly serve
others and build His kingdom.

So if you're still standing at that crossroad, what are you
waiting for? Muster your faith, take the leap, and stay the
course. I promise you that it will be worth it!

Father Is About Abundance

I have a friend, Karon Thackston, author of The Faith Process, who is a successful copywriter and marketing expert. Anything she takes on seems to prosper right out of the starting gate. I have been impressed with her ability to integrate her love for our Heavenly Father with her business practices and to lean on Him to guide her steps. As a result, He has prospered her greatly.

If one were to ask Karon to describe one attribute of our Heavenly Father, she would say, "Father never does anything small." Then she would quote Ephesians 3:20 and say that Father gives us "exceeding abundantly above all that we ask or think, according to the power that works in us." That power is the Spirit through our faith and our agency to choose.

Karon has a philosophy of abundance that is well-documented in scriptures. And I believe that this verse that Karon claims is a critical factor in her business success. She doesn't think small. Karon thinks big because she knows that Father thinks big. She knows that Heavenly Father wants to bless her. She follows the law of the tithe and accordingly the windows of heaven are opened and blessings are poured out upon her head (See Malachi 3:10).

Not only that, but Karon is a team player. She understands Luke 6:38, "Give, and it shall be given unto you; good measure, pressed down, and shaken together, and running over, shall men give into your bosom. For with the same measure that ye mete withal it shall be measured to you again."

A person who believes in abundance is willing to share what she has with others. She is willing to tithe, to donate to worthy causes, to give customers her very best, and to help others. This person knows that the laws of God dictate that those who give will have it returned to them in "good measure, pressed down, shaken together and running over."

People with scarcity mentalities limit their own ability to receive. Because they will not sow, they cannot reap. Jesus said, "The thief cometh not, but for to steal, and to kill, and to destroy: I am come that they might have life, and that they might have it more abundantly" (John 10:10).

Our Heavenly Father and His Son Jesus Christ want to bless us with abundance! When we obey God's laws we reap the natural consequences of those laws. When we receive any blessing, it is by obedience to that law upon which the blessing is predicated. Ignorance is no excuse. Just because a baby doesn't know about gravity doesn't keep gravity from acting upon him should he dive off a couch. Neither do the laws of God suspend themselves just because we aren't aware of them. As we study the word of God, we are led to understand important laws that govern God's universe. We learn that there is abundance in God's creations. The propensity to believe that God will deny us the things we need keeps us from obtaining all that He has to give us, because we're not exercising the faith necessary to receive.

We may ask, but do we really expect to receive? James 1:5-6 emphasizes this aspect of asking and receiving: "If any of you lack wisdom, let him ask of God which giveth to all men liberally and upbraideth not, and it shall be given him. But let him ask in faith, nothing wavering, for he that waverth is like a wave of the sea driven with the wind and tossed."

If there are things that are lacking in your life – whether they be spiritual or physical – begin to believe that your Heavenly Father has more than enough and to spare to fulfill your needs and desires. He wants to bless you. Seek to understand His will for your life, and then exercise your faith in accordance with His will to ask, and to believe that He will answer with abundance. Envision what you desire and thank Him in advance for what you know He will provide.

7 Greatest Gifts My Dad Ever Gave Me

Due to the level of family break-ups and divorce, more and more people today are being raised without the consistent influence of a good father. Many children are fortunate if they get to see their father every-other weekend. As I meet people who have grown up under these circumstances, my gratitude continues to grow for the fact that I had the blessed experience of being raised with my biological father not only in my home, but also as an active influence in my life.

My fondest memories of childhood are those hours I spent sitting on the couch with my father as he taught me how to read and how to do math problems or just asked my opinion on things. Although my father has his flaws, just like any mortal man would, I don't think I could have had a better father. I'd like to discuss 7 gifts my father gave that money cannot buy and nothing can replace – 7 gifts that made me who I am today – 7 gifts which I believe would cure a multitude of ills in our society.

His Time

My father spent hours with me teaching me, talking with me, and listening to me. It seemed as if we were inseparable. As a child I felt he belonged just to me because I got all the attention I needed.

Affection

All those nights he spent tickling my belly, playing his
harmonica or singing to me until I fell asleep are indelibly
imprinted in my mind. As a child I felt incredibly loved,
incredibly cared for. This foundation of affection built secu-
rity, stability and trust in the most formative years of my life.
Even at age 16, I remember my dad coming in my room when I
had my friends over and he'd chat with us for a few minutes.
As he'd leave I'd give him a kiss on his cheek. I remember one
friend saying, "You have such a great dad!" Even then, I
knew I did.

A Love of Learning

As I mentioned earlier, my dad spent many hours teaching me
how to read and do math. As young as the age of 3, he had me
reading the newspaper. He used to say he could give me
anything to learn and I'd learn it – no questions asked. He
said if he'd handed me a telephone book and said, "Memorize
this" I would have done it. I believe this is largely due to the
love, confidence and trust I had in my father. Whatever he
thought was worth learning, I knew must be worthwhile and
even fun.

Confidence

My dad actually raised me to be a bit of a show off and a ham-
bone. He was so thrilled that I could read and do math tricks
that he had me show them to everyone who came to the house.
And of course, a young child is going to be on cloud nine

when everyone starts ooh-ing and awe-ing over how smart she is. What confidence that built! To this day, I still have this compelling urge to take what I've learned and share it with others. And I largely attribute that level of confidence – the confidence to even *think* anything I'd have to say would be worthwhile to someone else – to my father's influence. So now you know who to blame for my verbosity.

Independence

My father had this habit of asking questions of us children. He'd ask me, "Marnie, would you rather be the smartest girl in school or the prettiest girl in school?" Whatever I said was ok, but whenever I gave the better answer, he'd say, "You know, I think you're right. I think you're onto something there." Our opinions were always valued and never belittled – even if they weren't exactly what he wanted to hear. But he always subtly reinforced the opinions we had that were sound and worthwhile. My father truly believes that children are smarter than most adults are. He honestly valued our opinions. This kind of unconditional respect enabled me to think for myself. I had literally no desire to conform to the crowd as a child or teenager. I virtually did not even know the meaning of the term "peer pressure." This gift of independent thinking allowed me to stand up for what was right even when it may have been unpopular.

Trust

My dad trusted us implicitly. If we were out at night, he only asked that we call in if we were going to be late so that he wouldn't worry that we had been in a car wreck. He trusted us to do the right thing, and because we knew he trusted us, we would never want to let him down.

Love of Country and Freedom

My father is a true patriot, a friend to freedom. He taught us to love and understand the Constitution of the United States and instilled in us the ability to determine which laws or candidates were constitutionally sound and those that were not. He sees freedom as our most treasured gift from God, and taught us that freedom is protected and fostered when we make right choices and give other people that same freedom. We cannot build our own freedom by taking away the freedom of another individual.

I am convinced if every child had a father who gave her these 7 gifts, many problems would be solved in our society. I myself have fallen woefully short in passing these gifts on to my own children. Yet the older I get and the more I learn about the problems faced by individuals in our society, the more I can trace my happiness and success in life back to these seven priceless gifts. I just hope it is not too late for me to start passing them on to my own children.

What I Learned About God from Being a Parent

Often when things haven't gone my way, I've exhibited some of the characteristics of our children and teens. As I've caught myself in the act, I've realized that God probably doesn't appreciate my behavior any more than I cherish that of my children.

But I've Made Plans!

When young people – teens in particular - are being disciplined or just when parents won't let them do what they want to do, they sometimes say, "You hate me. You don't love me." Corrections and restrictions hurt our feelings – especially when we're convinced that the plans we've laid are the best. "But, Mom, you can't say no. I've already arranged everything. Johnny's mom can pick me up to spend the night and she said she'd bring me back tomorrow," a child might reason. Likewise, the Lord might say "no" even when we've made elaborate plans, everything's fallen into place and we've given a sigh of relief that everything is now perfect. Just about then, the other shoe drops. "Forget your plans," a wise Heavenly Father says, "I've got something better in mind for you." Or, "You need to learn this lesson right now… it will be important later on."

When the Lord says, "No" or cancels our plans, He's not saying, "You're on my black list." He's saying, "I've got better plans for you" or "It's time to learn something new."

As Proverbs 3:5-7 says, "Trust in the LORD with all thine heart; and lean not unto thine own understanding. In all thy ways acknowledge Him, and He shall direct thy paths. Be not wise in thine own eyes: fear the LORD, and depart from evil." Sometimes "there is a way which seemeth right unto a man, but the end thereof are the ways of death" (Proverbs 14:12).

Gimme, Gimme, Gimme

Every parent knows what it's like to buy your child what she wants at the store and then no sooner than she's walked through the threshold of your home, she's tossed that toy aside and began to beg for the next one she just saw on a commercial. This particularly annoys me – no gratitude, just "Gimme more. Buy me more." How do you think it makes Heavenly Father feel when He gives us our request, and then we just briefly take advantage of it, showing little or no gratitude and come begging for more?

Temper Tantrums

Little Jenny isn't getting her way. She lays on the floor, kicks, screams, and demands what she wants. How inclined is her mother to give her what she wants? If mother is weak and worn, she may give in just to keep Jenny quiet. But if it's a refreshed or resolute mother, then there's no way little Jenny's getting what she's screaming for – not until she settles down and politely says "please." This is a big thing around our house. If you want something, don't come demanding or accusing, "You didn't get me a cookie!" – especially when you never even politely asked for one first. How many times do our prayers turn into demands and temper tantrums instead of respectful requests for help?

I Want it NOW!

I'll never forget the day I was taking Jillian to the doctor for her physical to start kindergarten. She knew she needed to visit the doctor to start school and she was excited to start. But she didn't realize that she would receive four shots and a prick on her finger. The appointment wasn't until the afternoon, but first thing in the morning, Jillian was dressed, ready to go and hanging on the door knob, "When are we gonna go? I wanna go! Let's goooooo, Mom!"

I kept telling her that there was no point leaving early, that we wouldn't see the doctor any sooner, and we'd just be bored waiting in the doctor's office. I explained that she could play or watch a video here at home until it was time to go. My logic wasn't getting through. On and on she went. She made absolutely no use of the time before the appointment — which means I didn't either. Finally, we did leave earlier than planned and of course wasted time in the waiting room.

Just like Jillian we rush our lives away, wasting time griping about having to wait instead of making use of the interim for better things. Nothing changes the appointed time of the Lord – not even our whining. Jeremiah lamented that people were not as bright as animals in understanding the Lord's timing, "Yea, the stork in the heaven knoweth her appointed times; and the turtle and the crane and the swallow observe the time of their coming; but my people know not the judgment of the Lord" (Jeremiah 8:7).

By being a parent, I've learned to appreciate my Heavenly Father and His long-suffering for us. I even cringe now and then when I catch myself acting like a tantrum-throwing-two-year-old or a teenager with a paranoid martyr complex. Even my attempts to be "adult" and reason with Him about how my plans would really be the best or my timing is better than His, are still too much like a certain kindergartner who obliviously rushed to get her four shots and a finger prick.

I know it's probably fruitless to second guess what Heavenly Father is really up to in our lives, but there is a little game I like to play when I catch myself acting like a child. I try to guess what He will do… how this current inconvenience could all miraculously work out for my good and teach me something very important. Of course the odds of me guessing correctly are remote, but at least the game changes my perspective to one of submission instead of defiance and humility instead of pride. Give it a try the next time you catch yourself acting like a two-year-old or teen.

Are We Really Free?

While pondering the 5th chapter of Isaiah, a few verses stood out to me:

"Woe unto them that rise up early in the morning, that they may follow strong drink; that continue until night, till wine inflame them! And the harp and the viol, the tabret, and the pipe, and wine, are in their feasts: but they regard not the work of the Lord, neither consider the operation of his hands. Therefore my people are gone into captivity, because they have no knowledge: and their honorable men are famished, and their multitude dried up with thirst" (verses 11-13).

"Woe unto them that call evil good, and good evil; that put darkness for light, and light for darkness; that put bitter for sweet, and sweet for bitter! Woe unto them that are wise in their own eyes, and prudent in their own sight!" (verses 20-21)

My first thought is that this passage sounds like many people today – more concerned with pleasures of the world, working for the weekend, partying, caring nothing for the things of God, having no regard for His work, or knowledge of Him or His words. There's definitely much of this kind of living going on in the world today.

But upon closer inspection, as I read these verses again and wrote them down, a second layer of wisdom leapt from the pages. I love the words of Isaiah for this very reason. He offers such rich treasures of knowledge – layers upon layers of meaning particularly for us today.

Notice the pattern here with the people that Isaiah is describing:

They concentrate on the body and its appetites. These people are drinking and partying and heavily involved in things that excite the senses. They live to feed and arouse their physical desires while numbing their consciences.

They ignore spiritual things. They have no regard for the things of the Lord. They don't consider the operation of His hands. They totally disregard the things of the spirit.

They fall into captivity because they have no knowledge. Are these people illiterate? Are they lacking scientific knowledge? Not necessarily because verse 21 says they are "wise in their own eyes and prudent in their own sight." These people have fallen into captivity because they have no knowledge of spiritual things. They do not know God or how He operates. A lack of spiritual knowledge brings people into bondage and captivity.

Captivity takes many forms. Ultimately captivity becomes political oppression such as subjection to dictators, socialism, communism or fascist rule. This type of captivity typically results from ignorance of political systems, history, and the principles of freedom. Although not all civilizations have been brought into captivity because of disregard for God and spiritual things, many have. There are other types of captivity as well. We can be in bondage to addictions (as described in Isaiah). We can be enslaved to bad habits, time-wasting activities, guilt, self-pity, immorality, material possessions, and our own pride and vanity.

They are spiritual starved. "Their honorable men are famished, and their multitude dried up with thirst." No matter how much scientific knowledge or worldly wisdom we think we have, if we ignore God and His operations and focus on our physical wants, needs and desires, we'll still be unsatisfied. A gnawing underlying hunger and thirst that cannot be filled will plague us. As a society (as a multitude) we are dried up with thirst. Our world is fast becoming a spiritual vacuum. No amount of technology or scientific discovery can compensate for spiritual starvation.

We live in a society where people "call evil good, and good evil; and put darkness for light, and light for darkness; that put bitter for sweet, and sweet for bitter." Political correctness and social acceptability have become the new religion. How many times on the nightly news have you seen the "wicked justified" and spin doctors, "take away the righteousness of the righteous from him?" (Isaiah 5:23)

What is the result of this kind of disregard for spiritual things? Captivity – spiritual and physical captivity, spiritual death, and ultimately political captivity. As mentioned earlier, captivity comes from a lack of knowledge. What knowledge? We fall into captivity when we have no knowledge of the principles of freedom. Where do these principles of freedom come from? 2 Corinthians 3:17 teaches us that "where the Spirit of the Lord is, there is liberty." The opposite is true as well. There can be no liberty where there is no Spirit of the Lord. We cannot expect to have the Spirit of the Lord with us

to direct, guide, protect and keep us free if we have no knowledge of spiritual things.

Freedom, contrary to the world's philosophy, is not the license
to do whatever feels good. Freedom cannot exist without
responsibility. Rights cannot exist without responsibility. You
can't have ultimate spiritual and physical freedom without
God – the author of liberty. We cannot continue to ignore God
and expect to be free.

George Mason, the Father of the Bill of Rights explained, "As
nations cannot be rewarded or punished in the next world, so
they must be in this. By an inevitable chain of causes and
effects, Providence punishes national sins by national
calamities."

Psalms 33:12 states, "Blessed is the nation whose God is the
Lord." And Proverbs 14:34 tells us that "Righteousness
exalteth a nation; but sin is a reproach to any people." "But
the nation and kingdom that will not serve [God] shall perish;
yea, those nations shall be utterly destroyed" (Isaiah 60:12).
Let us work to turn the tide – to wake up our fellow beings to a
sense of their awful situation. Society cannot continue to
ignore God and expect to find happiness or receive anything
but a gnawing, plaguing thirst that cannot be quenched with
any amount of physical stimulation or substance abuse.

The only way to quench this thirst is to turn to the One who
has the living waters of which, if men drink, they shall never
thirst. Jesus told the woman at the well, "But whosoever
drinketh of the water that I shall give him shall never thirst;

but the water that I shall give him shall be in him a well of water springing up into everlasting life" (John 4: 14). It is the knowledge of our Heavenly Father, of Jesus Christ, and of how the Holy Spirit operates that we must obtain in order to enjoy freedom. We must study God's words, hold fast to it, pray, ask, seek and act upon what we have learned. Knowledge is gained by not only studying, but also by doing. As we put His words into action, we learn by experience that the truth shall truly make us free. (John 8:32)

The Perfect Law of Liberty

What is freedom? Is freedom the license to do whatever you want, whenever you want without worrying about consequences? Are there or should there be limits on freedom? Does it have boundaries?

According to Merriam-Webster's Collegiate Dictionary, freedom is "the absence of necessity, coercion, or constraint in choice or action." So when our ability to choose becomes limited by others or ourselves we experience a loss of freedom. Many in the world today believe that religious morality enslaves and limits freedom. They believe that subjecting oneself to the Ten Commandments is binding and restrictive.

No one compels us to live The Ten Commandments. We are free to choose whether we will accept and abide by them or not. If we choose to follow them, we are promised that the Lord's Spirit will be with us. And "where the Spirit of the Lord is, there is liberty" (2 Corinthians 3: 17). We are all free to choose to keep the commandments of God, have His Spirit to be with us, and thus have liberty or we can choose to break His commandments, be devoid of His Spirit and be in bondage. As Galatians 5:1 explains, "Stand fast therefore in the liberty wherewith Christ hath made us free, and be not entangled again with the yoke of bondage."

One might ask, how is breaking God's commandments bondage? After all, isn't the person who does not bind himself by the command, "thou shalt not commit adultery" freer than the person who chooses not to bind himself by that commandment? He may feel "freer" in the moment of decision and action, but when the natural consequences of the choice begin to unfold, bondage is the result. The person who chooses to be faithful to his spouse experiences the liberating consequences of love, trust, faithfulness, devotion and peace of mind. The person who chooses to violate this commandment faces guilt, loss of trust, heartbreak, shattered homes, scarred children, and more. In the end, who is more "constrained in their future choices or actions" – the adulterer or the faithful spouse?

Peter seemed to have forseen our day when he spoke of those who would "speak great swelling words of vanity" and "allure through the lusts of the flesh through much wantonness." He warned that these people would "promise liberty" while "they themselves are the servants of corruption." Those who are overcome by these temptations are "brought into bondage."

He goes on to explain that if those who have had a knowledge of the Lord and Savior Jesus Christ and have escaped the pollutions of the world, then become again entangled in worldly activities, the "end is worse with them than the beginning." He says, "For it had been better for them not to have known the way of righteousness, than, after they have known it, to turn from the holy commandment delivered unto them. But it is happened unto them according to the true proverb, The dog is turned to his own vomit again; and the sow that was washed to her wallowing in the mire" (2 Peter 2:18-22).

There is no one more foolish than someone who once enjoyed the companionship of the Holy Ghost, but who has now lost it is. The Spirit of the Lord will not always strive with men and women (Genesis 6:3). We must choose to have it with us, and if we choose to do things that drive the Spirit away, we self-destruct. It's amazing what horribly poor choices we make when we are devoid of the Spirit of God – especially after once enjoying that Spirit. I believe this is why Peter says we had been better off if we had never known the way.

On the other hand, "whoso looketh into the perfect law of liberty, and continueth therein, he being not a forgetful hearer, but a doer of the work, this man shall be blessed in his deed." James 1: 25

We are all free to choose liberty and eternal life through our great Mediator Jesus Christ or captivity and death through Satan, the master of deception. Each of us is faced with choices every day. Some lead us up and some lead us down, but with each choice we make we either expand or limit our future choices. We are free to choose, but we are not free to choose consequences. The consequence of violating God's laws is a loss of freedom in future choices. It is much like the old saying, "What a tangled web we weave…" One lie, one broken commandment, one poor choice leads to another and then another, until we are completely entangled in a web of our own making. We create our own punishment through the natural consequences of our own poor choices.

The choices we make with our own limited and finite mortal minds quickly lead us away from freedom into slavery. Let us strive to have the Spirit of the Lord with us. With the ex-panded view of the Spirit, we can make wise choices that lead to more freedom and happiness than we could ever achieve on our own.

By Their Fruits
Ye Shall Know Them

As I was reading through Matthew chapter 10, which records Jesus calling his twelve apostles and telling them of their duties and the unpopularity they would face, I wondered what Jesus would say about being politically correct in today's world. He warned his disciples that they would be brought before governors and kings, that they would be hated for His name's sake, that they would be persecuted and flee from city to city. He told them that just as people said he was of the house of Beelzebub (the devil), the world will also call them (his divinely ordained apostles) of Satan's household. It doesn't sound like his disciples where very "PC."

I am reminded of something my dad has always said, "If the world loves you, then you must be doing something wrong. And if they hate you, you must be doing something right." Although this statement isn't always true, it does hold much of the time. Goodness and truth are rarely popular in the eyes of the world. Many times those who are most persecuted are they who are closest to the Savior, whereas those who are lauded as wonderful are often those who deny Him and promote Satan's agenda.

It is not what people say about us that matters, it is who we are inside and the fruit we bear. In Matthew 7:16-20, Jesus gave us the true test of any belief, doctrine, principle, idea or person:

"Ye shall know them by their fruits. Do men gather grapes of thorns, or figs of thistles? Even so every good tree bringeth forth good fruit; but a corrupt tree bringeth forth evil fruit. A good tree cannot bring forth evil fruit, neither can a corrupt tree bring forth good fruit. Every tree that bringeth not forth good fruit is hewn down, and cast into the fire. Wherefore by their fruits ye shall know them."

Beliefs determine actions. So, we can determine the value of any principle, belief or idea by looking at the results of it in the lives of those who practically apply it (not just those who claim to). What we have to ask ourselves when judging something is whether it bears good fruit or not. How popular, socially acceptable or how politically correct it is, is irrelevant. Actions speak louder than words. The following series of questions prove helpful when judging the fruit of any principle, doctrine or belief:

When properly applied, does it lead to

- more good or more evil?
- more closeness or distance from Jesus Christ?
- more light or more darkness?
- more truth or more error?
- more peace or more confusion?
- more happiness or more misery?
- more friendship or more animosity?
- more love or more hate?

We must be careful that we do not judge that which is good and from God to be evil or that which is of Satan to be good. Isaiah warned us, "Woe unto them that call evil good, and good evil; that put darkness for light, and light for darkness;

that put bitter for sweet, and sweet for bitter!" (Isaiah 5:20).
We live in a world that does much of this.

How do we live in a world that calls good evil?

It's tough living in a world that calls good evil and evil good –
especially when you're trying to live your life on the good
side, and even moreso when you haven't been taught correct
principles. But Christ gives us several ways to cope with this
in Matthew 10.

Be Wise, Yet Harmless

Christ told his disciples, "I send you forth as sheep in the
midst of wolves: be ye therefore wise as serpents and harmless
as doves" (Matthew 10:16). True wisdom comes from God. We
must work to have His Spirit with us at all times so we can be
wise in distinguishing truth from error and so that we do not
mistakenly call evil good or good evil. For the Holy Ghost, the
Comforter, is the spirit of truth and by the power of the Holy
Ghost you may know the truth of all things. (John 15:26)

Let the Spirit Guide

Jesus told his disciples, "Take no thought how or what ye
shall speak: for it shall be given you in that same hour what
ye shall speak. For it is not ye that speak, but the Spirit of your
Father which speaketh in you" (Matthew 10:19-20). John
14:26 also tells us that "the Comforter, which is the Holy
Ghost, whom the Father will send in my name, he shall teach
you all things, and bring all things to your remembrance,
whatsoever I have said unto you."

For something to be remembered, we need to study. Study the scriptures. Feed good things into your mind. Then when you're called upon to defend your beliefs or bear testimony of what you know is true the Spirit can bring those things to your remembrance and also inspire you to say something you never even thought of before.

Fear Not

Matthew 10:26 says that when they call us of the devil or evil because of our beliefs, we should, "Fear them not, for there is nothing covered, that shall not be revealed; and hid, that shall not be known." The truth will be known one day. We must "fear not them which kill the body, but are not able to kill the soul: but rather fear him which is able to destroy both soul and body in hell" (v28). It is our soul that matters not how popular we are or even what others may do to our very lives. In the end, it is what we do with our souls that matters.

Remember You Have Value

Jesus tells us that the very hairs of our head are numbered. If not even a sparrow falls to the ground without our Father noticing, how much more value are we than many sparrows? (v30-32). We have great value in the eyes of God.

Put God First

Jesus says in Matthew 10:37, "He that loveth father or mother more than me is not worthy of me: and he that loveth son or daughter more than me is not worthy of me. And he that taketh not his cross, and followeth after me, is not worthy of me. He that findeth his life shall lose it: and he that loseth his life for my sake shall find it."

From an Old Testament perspective we might say that God wants us to put him first because he is a jealous God and wants to be uppermost in our minds. But, from a New Testament perspective, I have come to understand that he loves us so much that he knows that the only way we can truly reach our full potential is to put him first. We have to keep our eye on the goal. God grants us according to the desires of our hearts. "For where your treasure is, there will your heart be also" (Matthew 6:21).

We have to truly **want** to follow him. It's not an easy or popular path. Until and unless we are willing to forget worrying about what other people think of us, we will not have the desire or the courage to do what truly needs to be done to become all that he has in store for us. We cannot find ourselves — our true potential until we are willing to lose the life we have artificially made for ourselves.

So the next time you feel attacked for your beliefs, draw on these tips the Savior gave us. Or the next time you see someone attacked for their beliefs, take a good hard look. Pay less attention to what their attackers say and look closely at the fruit. When carefully observed, do the beliefs in question lead to do good and to believe in Christ? If so, then you know they come from God. If not, you know they don't.

Building Your Temple: Be Strong and Do It!

In 1 Chronicles chapter 28 King David turns over his kingdom along with all the materials he had gathered for building the temple to his son Solomon. David had hoped that he would be able to build the temple according to the plans which the Lord had given him through the spirit, but that was not to be. The Lord told David, "Thou shalt not build an house for my name because thou… hast shed blood." David had Uriah sent to the forefront of battle so that he would be killed in order to cover up an adulterous relationship which David had with Uriah's wife. David's sin kept him from being worthy to build a temple to God. And so that honor fell upon David's son Solomon.

The Lord declared that Solomon had been chosen and that he should sit on the throne and build the temple. David gave Solomon the patterns for every aspect of the temple along with all the materials down to the gold for candlesticks and meat hooks. Everything Solomon needed was there along with the priests and men who would build the temple.

Plant Good Thoughts

Along with the materials and patterns, David gave his son two pieces of advice. First he said, "Solomon, my son, know thou the God of thy fathers and serve him with a perfect heart and with a willing mind: for the Lord searcheth all hearts, and understandeth all the imaginations of the thoughts: if thou seek him, he will be found of thee; but if thou forsake him, he will cast thee off forever."

David was speaking from experience here. He had sought the Lord with his thoughts and desires and he had found Him. But there were other thoughts that plagued David – lustful desires that came forward into adulterous actions, an illegitimate child, and eventual murder. David is the one who taught Solomon by word and poor example that "as a man thinketh in his heart so is he" (Proverbs 23:7). The thoughts and imaginations of the heart crystallize into words and actions. Perhaps this is why Jesus taught that "every idle word that men shall speak, they shall give account thereof in the day of judgment" (Matthew 12:36). That's a strong statement! Words indicate the thoughts of the heart. Jesus said, "A good man out of the good treasure of his heart bringeth forth that which is good; and an evil man out of the evil treasure of his heart bringeth forth that which is evil: for of the abundance of the heart his mouth speaketh" (Luke 6:45).

Thoughts lead to words which eventually lead to actions. Think of thoughts as seeds that eventually sprout into our words and bear fruit in actions. This is why Jesus could say, "That whosoever looketh on a woman to lust after her hath committed adultery with her already in his heart" (Matthew 5:28). The seed has been planted, and spiritually speaking the action or thing is created the minute we imagine it in our thoughts.

Knowing this, we realize that we must do more than bite our tongues, we must also control our thoughts! In her book, "Me and My Big Mouth," Joyce Myer says that if we carried a tape recorder around on our belt and recorded some of the things we say, we would be shocked at our negativity. She said we'd hear things like,

"'This kid of mine is never going to change. I may as well forget it – the more I pray the worse he acts.'

'This marriage is just simply not going to work out. I absolutely cannot put up with any more of this. I am going to leave if one more thing happens. If necessary, I will get a divorce.'

'It never fails. Every time I get a little money, some disaster comes along and takes it all away.'

'I just can't hear from God; He never speaks to me.'

'Nobody loves me. It looks like I am destined to be lonely all my life.'

Yet at the same time we are making such negative statements, we claim that we are believing for our children, our marriages, and our finances, that we are believing to be led by the Spirit and to find our lifetime mate"[1]

If we expect better things in our lives, then we need to be thinking better thoughts and speaking positive things. **In life, we don't get what we want; we get what we expect in our hearts!**

Don't Give Up, You're Not Alone

The second piece of advice David gave Solomon was "Be strong and of a good courage and do it: fear not, nor be dismayed: for the Lord God, even my God will be with thee; he will not fail thee, nor forsake thee, until thou has finished all the work for the service of the house of the Lord" (1 Chronicles 28:20).

Be strong, be courageous, DO IT! You're not alone. That's advice that we all can take. When the Lord gives you a message, a direction or a plan, lay aside your fears and just DO IT. The Lord will not fail you nor forsake you. All of the work necessary will be completed according to God's plan and in His time.

There is so much rich symbolism in the story of Solomon's temple that we can apply to accomplishing anything that the Lord has asked us to do – any righteous desire of our hearts.

1. **It all starts with a thought** – an idea or plan given by the Spirit. (1 Chronicles 28:12)
2. **Give it time** When you start out, you'll rarely have everything you need to make the plan a reality. You'll need to gather materials, relationships and experience just as David gathered materials for the temple.
3. **You must remain faithful** or someone else may be called to finish what you started. (1 Chronicles 28:3-4)
4. **Write down your plans**. A goal that isn't written is simply a wish. (1 Chronicles 28:11-12,19)
5. **Support your plan with your thoughts** Use the thoughts and imaginations of your heart to envision your objective

and keep a positive, faithful frame of mind that feeds your plan. (1 Chronicles 28:9)

6. **Be Strong and Do it. The Lord is on your side** (1 Chronicles 28:10, 20). The Lord will not fail you nor forsake you throughout the entire process.

Together, we are co-creators with God. When we have a righteous idea or plan that He is in agreement with, nothing is impossible for us. We have access to His grace – His full power to bring everything we need – all the materials, knowledge and experience into our grasp so that if we are faithful, courageous, and *do it*, we will not fail!

1) Joyce Meyer, *Me and My Big Mouth: Your Answer Is Right Under Your Nose*, p 54-58.

There Is a Time for Every Purpose and Every Work

"To everything there is a season and a time for every purpose under the heaven" says Ecclesiastes 3:1. While reading this chapter of Ecclesiastes, a portion of verse 17 leapt out at me, "There is a time for every purpose and for every work."

Over the last few weeks, I've been able to almost-effortlessly turn some ideas I had two years ago into a reality. I'm an idea person and have more ideas than I know what to do with. I easily become overwhelmed and run around like a chicken with its head cut off trying to do too many things at once. My former coach encouraged me to create a master list of ideas so that they were recorded for later reference. I've kept up this practice off-and-on over the last few years and when the opportunity and knowledge presented itself to turn those old ideas into a reality, I learned an important lesson.

Sometimes God gives us ideas whose time has not yet come. For example, many times ideas come to me with such force and in such a burst of light and knowledge that I know they didn't come from within me. There's no doubt that they came from God. I recognize these ideas because they fill me with joy. They are filled with light. But often, I become so frustrated because at the time they come, I may not have the means or the knowledge to make them a reality. So reluctantly I file the idea back into a corner of my mind and eventually the time, season and purpose for that work presents itself.

This most recent instance arose when there was a programming problem on one of my Web sites that required me to act quickly, research a solution and repair the problem. In my moment of need, the Lord led me to a piece of programming code that not only fixed the current problem, but also gave me the knowledge to quickly and easily implement the ideas He gave me two years ago. Within a week's time those ideas became a reality. They were there waiting for their time and their purpose.

What I learned from this experience is that we need not question the inspiration or answers we receive because the way or means to accomplish them are not immediately available. Sometimes the Lord gives us this insight so we

1. Have a direction to pursue,
2. Accumulate the knowledge and experience the idea requires, and
3. Can be on the lookout for the opportunity when the perfect time arises – even when that opportunity is hidden within a crisis.

We need not be discouraged because we can't do everything we want to do right now. We can take comfort in knowing that the Lord has a time and a purpose for every righteous desire that He puts within our hearts.

The hard part for us humans is having the patience to wait for God's perfect timing. We often try to force the issue. But our own efforts to manipulate a situation to change the foreordained timing of events will only end in frustration. In God's timing, events just flow. I can always recognize when the timing is off by when I'm having to work too hard to make things happen. That's a sure sign that God's telling me to wait for the right moment.

From now on, I will remember that the timing of inspiration and fruition don't always coincide. I will console myself in knowing that the inspiration and vision He showers my way today will eventually become a reality - even if it's in a distant tomorrow. I'll better document enlightenment as it comes, and praise Him when its season arrives.

All Things Work Together for Good

"And we know that all things work together for good to them that love God, to them who are the called according to his purpose" (Romans 8:28).

A classic example of this verse at work is the life of Joseph who was sold into Egypt by his brothers. Joseph endured many hardships. His brothers hated him because he was his father's favorite. Some of his brothers wanted to kill him, but they ended up selling him into slavery. He was taken to Egypt where he was falsely accused of sinning with his master's wife. He was thrown into prison where he stayed until he interpreted a dream for a butler and a baker. Their dreams came true and the butler promised to tell Pharaoh about Joseph and his ability to interpret dreams, but the butler forgot until two more years had passed.

Finally when the Pharaoh had his own dream that needed interpreting, the butler remembered and told Pharaoh about Joseph. At a glance, it would appear that Joseph couldn't win for losing, but no matter where he was planted, he always flourished. And there's no evidence that he ever complained.

In his first stop at Potiphar's house, Joseph found grace in Potiphar's sight and Potiphar made Joseph overseer over his house. "The Lord blessed the Egyptian's house for Joseph's sake; and the blessings of the Lord was upon all that he had in the house, and in the field" (See Genesis 39:3-7).

When Potiphar's wife tried to seduce Joseph, so swift was his flight that he left his garment behind in her hands. In her anger, she told Potiphar that Joseph had attacked her, and the garment was proof. Potiphar believed his wife and threw Joseph in prison.

But even in prison, Joseph prospered. "The Lord was with Joseph, and showed him mercy, and gave him favor in the sight of the keeper of the prison. And the keeper of the prison committed to Joseph's hand all the prisoners that were in the prison; and whatsoever they did there, he was the doer of it. The keeper of the prison looked not to anything that was under his hand; because the Lord was with him, and that which he did, the Lord made to prosper" (Genesis 39:21-23).

When the butler finally remembered Joseph, and Pharaoh called for him, Pharaoh said, "I have heard say of thee, that thou canst understand a dream to interpret it." But Joseph gave God the glory and replied, "It is not in me: God shall give Pharaoh an answer of peace." As a consequence of Joseph using his God-given gift to bless others, Pharaoh put him in charge of all the land of Egypt. "Pharaoh took off his ring from his hand, and put it upon Joseph's hand, and arrayed him in vestures of fine linen, and put a gold chain about his neck. And he made him ride in the second chariot, which he had; and they cried before him, Bow the knee: and he made him ruler over all the land of Egypt" (Genesis 41:41-43).

Pharaoh's dream foretold of seven years of plenty followed by seven years of famine. Because of Joseph's interpretation and wise council to Pharaoh, Joseph was made governor over the

land and it was he that sold to all the people of the land.
(Genesis 42:6) When Joseph's father sent his brothers into
Egypt to buy grain, Joseph recognized them, although they
didn't recognize him. Through a series of interesting events,
Joseph tested his brothers to see if they had learned their
lesson. Joseph learned that his brothers still felt guilty for
what they had done to him. (Genesis 42:21-22)

When Joseph finally revealed his identity to his brothers, it
was evident that Joseph had forgiven them and saw the good
in the events of his life. He said, "Be not grieved, nor angry
with yourselves, that ye sold me hither: for God did send me
before you to preserve life. For these two years hath the famine
been in the land: and yet there are five years, in the which
there shall neither be earing nor harvest. And God sent me
before you to preserve you posterity in the earth, and to save
your lives by a great deliverance. So now it was not you that
sent me hither, but God: and he hath made me a father to
Pharaoh, and lord of all his house and a ruler throughout all
the land of Egypt" (Genesis 45:8).

Joseph loved the Lord and was obedient; therefore he reaped
the blessings of obedience and all things worked together for
his good. Contrast Joseph with Reuben. Reuben was the eldest
brother and should have had the birthright, but he lost it
because of his sin (Genesis 35:22). When his father gave his
final blessing upon his sons, he told Reuben, "thou art my
firstborn, my might, and the beginning of my strength...
unstable as water, thou shalt not excel" (Genesis 49:3-4).
Water seeks the lowest level. It goes with the flow. Reuben
gave into temptation with one of his father's wives. He gave in
to his brothers when they wanted to hide the fact that they

had sold Joseph into slavery. Reuben never learned to do what was right and let the consequence follow. And in the end, Joseph received the birthright from his father in Reuben's place.

Joseph was promised, "Joseph is a fruitful bough, even a fruitful bough by a well; whose branches run over the wall: The archers have sorely grieved him, and shot at him, and hated him; But his bow abode in strength, and the arms of his hands were made strong by the hands of the mighty God of Jacob; (from thence is the shepherd, the stone of Israel) Even by the God of thy father, who shall help thee; and by the Almighty, who shall bless thee with blessings of heaven above, blessings of the deep that lieth under... The blessings of thy father have prevailed above the blessings of my progenitors unto the utmost bound of the everlasting hills: they shall be on the head of Joseph, and on the crown of the head of him that was separate from his brethren" (Genesis 49:22-26).

Joseph and his posterity received the covenant blessings of Abraham, Isaac and Jacob. They receive them because Joseph was faithful, trustworthy and true no matter what adversity befell him. Like Joseph, if we put the Lord first, stay away from temptation and seek to give God the glory, all things will work together for our good as well. It may not be immediately obvious. It may take time – even years as in the case of Joseph. But if we trust in the Lord, look for the good, and follow His commandments, we will flourish even amidst adversity.

Trust the Choice Points:
The Story of Esther

Are you familiar with Esther? Is there a story in scripture more froth with twists, turns and ironies than the book of Esther? Her story makes it so easy to see how a life can be shaped not only by one's own decisions, but also by those of others, and that God is always at the helm.

As a bit of a refresher if you haven't read it in a while, Esther lived in the land ruled by Ahasuerus, king of Persia and Media. In the book of Esther, Ahasuerus has a great banquet and requests that his wife Vashti come to the banquet so everyone can see how beautiful she is. But Vashti decides she doesn't want to come and refuses to show. The king is furious and his servants suggest that the queen's insolence will incite women throughout the kingdom to be insubordinate to their husbands. So the servant suggests that Vashti be made a public example to show the women of the kingdom that they better listen to their husbands. The king agrees, Vashti is dethroned, and the young women of the land are gathered for the king to select a new queen.

Esther is brought by her uncle Mordecai to participate in this contest. Esther is so beautiful that she wins the heart of the king and is made the next queen in place of Vashti. But her uncle Mordecai tells her not to reveal that she is a Jew or that he is her uncle, so she doesn't. After Esther is made queen, Mordecai discovers a plot to kill the king and tells Esther about it. Esther informs the king and lets him know that it was Mordecai that learned of the plot. The conspirators are hanged and the whole incident is recorded in the king's chronicles.

Soon after, a conceited man named Haman is promoted to be the king's right-hand man. He makes everyone bow to him, but Mordecai won't. Haman is infuriated and talks the king into executing all the Jews because he says they are an insolent lot who refuse to obey the king's laws. The king gives Haman permission to do as he wishes with these people and a date is set to execute all the Jews.

Mordecai asks Esther to go before the king and plead for her people. There is a law that states if anyone comes before the king without being called, that the king can choose to execute them unless he decides to hold out his golden scepter to them. Esther is scared to go before the king, but Mordecai convinces her by saying, *"Think not with thyself that thou shalt escape in the king's house, more than all the Jews. If thou altogether holdest thy peace at this time, then shall there enlargement and deliverance arise to the Jews from another place: but thou and thy father's house shall be destroyed: and who knoweth whether thou art come to the kingdom for such a time as this?"* (Esther 4:13-14).

Esther asks all the people to fast and pray with her for 3 days and she goes before the king. The king extends his golden scepter in acceptance to her and grants her whatever she wishes. She invites the king and Haman to a special banquet. Haman is so excited that he is the only one besides the king invited to the banquet that he brags to his wife. The only fly in his ointment is that Mordecai still won't bow down to him. His wife says he shouldn't have to put up with that. He should build a gallows and hang Mordecai the next day before attending the queen's banquet. So Haman builds the gallows with the determination to hang Mordecai.

That night, the king can't sleep and asks that the chronicles of his kingdom be read to him. They read about Mordecai and how he helped reveal the plot against the king. "Has anyone rewarded Mordecai?" the king asks. No, he hasn't been rewarded for this. So the next day, the king brings Haman before him and asks him what would be the best way to honor someone. Haman, thinking the honor is for himself, describes how the king should lavishly reward someone. Much to his dismay, Haman is made to honor Mordecai in this lavish fashion.

Later that day, the king and Haman meet Esther for her banquet. The king asks Esther what she wishes of him and she tells him she wants the enemy who would destroy her and her people stopped. Who would do such harm to her and her people? Why, Haman! The king is incensed and commands that Haman should be hanged on the very gallows he designed to hang Mordecai upon. In the end, Mordecai becomes Haman's successor as the king's right-hand man, the Jews are spared and everyone lives happily ever after – except Haman and his family of course.

Think of all the choices that go into this story to make Esther's, Mordecai's, and Haman's lives unfold as they did. Even simple things like the king being unable to sleep and reading the chronicles drastically altered the fate of an entire nation. Have you ever thought back over your life to the road that led you where you are now? Have you ever stopped to identify the decisions and events that seemed insignificant at the time, but drastically altered the destination of your life? I call these "choice points."

This week I've reflected on the choice points that have led me to where I am today. Most seemed thoroughly insignificant or coincidental to me at the time. But, pull out any one of those choice points, and I would be a very different person, doing very different things with my life. I cannot help but marvel at the Lord's intricately laid plan for each of our lives. "The steps of a good man (or woman) are ordered by the LORD" (Psalm 37:23).

The Lord told Jeremiah, "Before I formed thee in the belly I knew thee; and before thou camest forth out of the womb I sanctified thee, and I ordained thee a prophet unto the nations" (Jeremiah 1:4-5). Just as Jeremiah was chosen before he was born and foreordained to be a prophet of God, each of us is here on earth at this time to fulfill a very special purpose – to fulfill a divine mission. It could be said of us as it was of Esther who was called to save her people from execution: "and who knoweth whether thou art come to the kingdom for such a time as this?" (Esther 4:14)

God has a plan for us that cannot be frustrated by our lack of talent, but He has given us our free will to choose to accept His plan for us or not. Esther could have said, "No, I'm too scared to go before the king." And as Mordecai said, the Lord would deliver the Jews another way, but what would have become of Esther?

With experience we learn to recognize the Lord's hand. We begin to sense the importance of life's twists and turns. In time, as we surrender to the Lord's will, we learn to trust the choice points – even the ones that are scary or sad. We come to know and to trust that even they will lead us to a better place.

I Stand at the Door and Knock

There is always a point where we have to let go. We work, we pray, we look forward to big events and life-changing experiences, but then there is always that point where we just have to let go and let time and events take their course. You can't control everything and that has always been one of my greatest challenges in life — letting go. There are so many things we **can** control in our lives that some of us feel we can simply **will** anything into existence, but this doesn't always work.

Probably the hardest challenge in letting go is when our goals, plans, and dreams involve other people. When our future is tied to someone else and s/he is unwilling or lacks the vision or courage to go where we want to go, what can we do? Do we halt our development and progression to wait on this other person to catch up? Do we run on and leave them behind? Or is there some other happy medium? We can't force someone else to see our vision, to follow our path. Arguing and pressuring only serve to drive them to dig in their heels, or worse, run in the opposite direction.

When we think of how God leads us in our lives, we find the answer. Firmness, not force is the key. God never gives in or wavers in his course, but he is long-suffering and ever-willing to take us back. We, as He, must be firm in our convictions, steadfast, focused and committed. Leading others up the path of truth requires love, patience, gentleness, diligence, meekness — and yes, time.

How many times have we messed up and Jesus is still there waiting and willing — standing at the door and knocking if we will but let him in? He never beats the door down. He never even picks the lock and sneaks in through manipulation. He doesn't shout, belittle or guilt-trip us from the other side of the door. He simply patiently stands there and knocks until the time arrives that we have the ears to hear the knocking and the willingness and courage to open the door.

Jesus knows that force, manipulation, power games, and dominion will never lead someone else to the light. Love, service, patient teaching and a good example will do more to soften hearts and shape lives than any argument or debate. Is someone else in your life that you love choosing the wrong paths? Are they digging in their heels when you would really like them to join you on your walk up the path of truth? Then, follow Christ's example. Be His partner in this endeavor. Be an instrument in his hands to help your friend or loved one hear the knocking. Take the time to teach them to listen and hear the tapping. When the time is right for them, take their hand and walk with them to open the door through which more joy and happiness than they ever dreamed possible exists.

The beautiful thing about this process is that as we strain to hear Christ at the door for our friend's sake, we hear Him ourselves. As we take our friend's hand to walk with them to the door we can't help but arrive at the door ourselves. And when our friend opens the door, we will be there to feel the flood of joy and happiness that flows as Christ enters.

When I Am Weak, I Am Strong: The Enabling Power of Grace

Probably one of the most powerful yet least understood principles of the gospel of Jesus Christ is that of grace. The Bible teaches that it is the merciful and compassionate grace of Jesus Christ that saves us. When we think of grace, we immediately think of our own inability to save ourselves and how far short we fall of perfection. This leads us to the realization that it is only by the grace of God that we can hope to inherit the kingdom of God.

Grace Justifies Us

In a court of law if someone is pronounced justified, he is pronounced "not guilty." He is proclaimed innocent. The only way for imperfect beings such as ourselves to be pronounced "not guilty" is by Someone else taking the blame for us – Someone else bearing the burden of our punishment. That Someone is Jesus Christ. It is His atoning grace that affords us this mercy when otherwise justice would take her exacting toll upon our souls. Speaking of the Savior, Ephesians 1:7 says, "In whom we have redemption through His blood, the forgiveness of sins, according to the riches of His grace" (See also Romans 3:24). His grace justifies us and makes us heirs with a hope of eternal life (See Titus 3:7). G.R.A.C.E. is an appropriate acronym for God's Riches At Christ's Expense.

Through Grace The Impossible Is Possible

But there is more to the concept of grace than meets the eye.
Grace is an enabling power. Jesus taught, "The things which
are impossible with men are possible with God" (Luke 18:27).
How are they possible? Through His grace! Grace is the
power by which God can work His will in our lives. It is the
power that allows ordinary people to do extraordinary things.

The concept of grace is outlined in Ephesians 2:8-10:

*"For by grace are ye saved through faith; and that not of yourselves:
it is the gift of God: Not of works, lest any man should boast. For we
are his workmanship, created in Christ Jesus unto good works,
which God hath before ordained that we should walk in them."*

Because on our own we fall miserably short, our works cannot
save us; but the purpose of God's grace is to recreate us in
Christ so that we can walk in good works. It is important to
note that God gives us grace so that we can do His works and
build His kingdom. A natural outflow of being in a state of
grace is an abundance of good works (also referred to as
"bearing fruit").

In the parable of the vine, Jesus explains that He is the true
vine and we are the branches. Those branches that do bear
fruit are purged so that they may bear even more fruit. Many
times the events that are most painful in our lives are God's
purging process enabling us to bear more fruit (do greater
works). Jesus said, *"Abide in me, and I in you. As the branch
cannot bear fruit of itself except it abide in the vine; no more can ye,*

except ye abide in me. I am the vine, ye are the branches: He that abideth in me, and I in him, the same bringeth forth much fruit; for without me ye can do nothing" (See John 15:1-7).

Without Christ's enabling grace, we can do nothing. With His grace, nothing that is God's will is impossible for us.

We are given grace that we might labor in the Lord's kingdom. "Let us have grace, whereby we may serve God" (Hebrews 12:28). Paul understood this principle, "But by the grace of God I am what I am: and his grace which was bestowed upon me was not in vain; but I labored more abundantly than they all: yet not I, but the grace of God which was with me" (1 Corinthians 15:10). Even though Paul labored for the Lord, he still recognized that the efficacy of his work was magnified far beyond his human capabilities because of the grace of Jesus Christ working through him. In other words, Paul was connected to the Vine, so he was bearing abundant fruit.

Where grace abounds, so abounds good works. (2 Corinthians 9:8) Grace enables ordinary individuals to do extraordinary things in the service of God.

Activating God's Grace

According to Paul, each of us has different God-given gifts distributed according to the grace that is given to us. We activate and magnify these gifts "according to the proportion of our faith" (Romans 12:6).

Faith in Jesus Christ is the beginning. Following faith is humility and repentance. James 4:6 says, "God resisteth the proud, but giveth grace unto the humble." We activate God's grace by recognizing our own nothingness, our own inability to solve our own problems. We must come to a point where we surrender our will to God's will – where we realize that His way is the blessed way. We must replace self-confidence with faith. The wonderful thing about grace is that it is irrelevant how talented, weak or human we may be, God's grace is sufficient to make us strong. If we lean only on ourselves, we see our own weakness and think, "I'll never be able to do that. I can't commit because I know I'm weak and I'll just mess up." But when we put our faith and trust in God, we can say, "Even though I am weak, I have faith that God will make me strong. I can do all things through Christ who strengthens me" (Philippians 4:13).

Because of and through our weaknesses, Christ can make us strong. Paul was plagued with what he referred to as a "thorn in the flesh." We don't know what it was. Perhaps it was guilty feelings over his past mistakes. Perhaps it was continual persecution, or maybe it was an illness that plagued him. He came to the Lord three times (most likely in three seasons of his life) and petitioned the Lord to remove this thorn in his flesh. But the Lord responded, "My grace is sufficient for thee: for my strength is made perfect in weakness." Paul continues, "Most gladly therefore will I rather glory in my infirmities, that the power of Christ may rest upon me. Therefore I take pleasure in infirmities, in reproaches, in necessities, in persecutions, in distresses for Christ's sake: **for when I am weak, then am I strong**" (2 Corinthians 12:7-10).

Paul received visions and revelations and was a great teacher, but he recognized that without this thorn in the flesh, he might have been tempted to be "exalted above measure." Therefore the Lord blessed Paul with humility by allowing him to suffer with this weakness.

It is in our extremities that we become humble enough to look to God and surrender to Him. It is when we wholeheartedly commit to Him and His will and surrender our control of the situation that we activate God's grace in our behalf. It is at this point that although we are weak, through Christ's grace we become strong.

As we replace self-confidence and our need-to-control with faith in the Lord Jesus Christ, we activate His powerful grace in our behalf. (Romans 12:3) With this grace, "no good thing will be withheld from us as we walk uprightly" (Psalms 84:11).

Grace "builds you up, and gives you an inheritance among all those who are sanctified" (Acts 20:32). "Let us therefore come boldly unto the throne of grace, that we may obtain mercy, and find grace to help in time of need" (Hebrews. 4: 16). Let us "grow in grace and in the knowledge of our Lord and Savior Jesus Christ" (2 Peter 3:18). As we lean on Him, our best efforts will no longer fall short because through the power of His grace, our weaknesses become strengths and the impossible becomes possible. Of this I leave my humble witness, that when we do our best to do God's will and lean on Christ's grace, He always makes up the difference.

Dig Your Holes
and Talk with Me

I'm putting in a fall garden this year and bought some
cauliflower, broccoli and cabbage plants to transplant.
Saturday morning I managed to sneak out of the house
without being followed by any of our six children. It was a
peaceful, cool morning as I carried my somewhat wilted
plants outside. I'd been so busy that I had neglected to water
them like I should. I turned on the water hose, but no water
came out. There wasn't even the typical sound of running
water. Normally, I would have gone inside the house to make
sure the water was working, but since I had escaped unno-
ticed, I didn't dare venture back into the house and interrupt
my few precious moments of solitude in the garden.

So I let a few dregs of water dribble out of the hose onto the
plants, and began digging holes for them. I'd worry about
finding the water for them later. I'm a hopper by nature, and
after digging a few holes, I was bored. Normally I would have
been turning the water on, filling the holes, transplanting a
few plants and then going back to digging. But this morning I
had no choice but to continue with the boring task of hole-
digging. I decided to use the time to talk with my Heavenly
Father. I began praying – just talking with Him really – and
thanking Him for all my wonderful blessings. I was marveling
aloud at how He had prepared so many things in advance for
me, before I knew I'd even need them.

Then, I asked Him about a challenge that's been perplexing
me. There is so much abundance in my life now – particularly

an abundance of opportunities – but not necessarily an abundance of resources to take advantage of those opportunities. There are some righteous desires that I have that are being halted due to lack of resources. I feel like I've set out a bunch of plants, but they aren't bearing fruit like they should. So I began to ask Him about this situation and what He'd like for me to do about it.

About this time, I'd dug all the holes I needed, so I went to a water hose on the other side of the house to see if it worked. It did, so I came back to the one closest to the garden and lo and behold, the water flowed freely. I carried the hose over to the garden and began to fill the holes with water. Then, the question forced its way out of my mouth, "Did You stop the water just so I would talk to You?"

The answer was "Yes." I believe that's not only why the water stopped for me that morning – so I'd take the time to talk with my Heavenly Father, but also why the symbolic water usually stops. Heavenly Father uses "lack" in our lives to get our attention – so that we'll talk with Him, so we'll listen to Him and most importantly ask Him questions.

There was so much symbolism in the garden experience that my mind began to whirl with the possibilities. First, I knew that my Heavenly Father was telling me that I'd been so busy lately that I'd neglected to *really* talk with Him. Oh, sure, I've had some short heartfelt prayers, but I hadn't taken the time to get by myself for any extended period of time and have a real conversation with Him.

Second, the water represented the Savior's "living waters" that bring life, nourishment, and abundance to any situation. It's so easy to get busy with tasks and forget that what really breathes life into any project is the "living waters" that flow from the Lord. My plants had already begun to wilt a little because I had neglected to water them. If they had been denied water long enough, they would have died. My efforts to dig the holes would have been in vain had the water been unavailable. The shock of putting them into dry soil without water would have killed them.

I began to see the parallels to my current situation. I may have some great projects going right now. I may be working hard and doing my part, but if I don't stay in constant communication with my Heavenly Father, the living waters will cease to flow and no amount of hard work, opportunities or resources can make up for a lack of living waters!

It's God's part of the formula that's missing. His message to me was, "Dig your holes and talk with me." How simple! Yet as humans we make it so hard. If we take Jesus at his literal word, we see just how simple this process is. In John 7:37-38 Jesus said, "If any man thirst, let him come unto me, and drink. He that believeth on me, as the scripture hath said, out of his belly shall flow rivers of living water."

To the woman at the well, He promised, "But whosoever drinketh of the water that I shall give him shall never thirst; but the water that I shall give him shall be in him a well of water springing up into everlasting life" (John 4:14).

Miracles happen where the living waters of inspiration flow. Everything lives and blooms with abundance, life and hope where the water flows. But cut off the living waters, and everything becomes barren and scarce.

Jesus taught that "blessed are all they who do hunger and thirst after righteousness, for they shall be filled [with the Holy Ghost]."

He also promised, "Ask, and it shall be given you; seek, and ye shall find; knock, and it shall be opened unto you: For every one that asketh receiveth; and he that seeketh findeth; and to him that knocketh it shall be opened" (Matthew 7:7-11).

The Lord wants to bless us with answers and with everything we need, but He wants us to remember to communicate with Him! Are you experiencing lack in your life? If so, how much gratitude are you expressing to your Heavenly Father for what He has given you? How is your communication with Him? Are you asking for guidance, expecting to obtain answers, or are you simply whining ungratefully? Are you talking with Him like you would a friend or have your prayers become ritualistic and redundant? Are you remembering to close your prayers in the name of Jesus Christ? Remember it's Christ who is your Advocate with the Father. Add power to your prayer by closing your prayer in His name. Are you listening? Are you taking some time away from TV, phones, computers and the noise of modern life to really listen? Take some time to commune with nature. In the world of His creations, He can talk with you and teach you what you need to know.

Another thing I noticed from my experience in the garden was
that I got my plants set in half the time it normally would have
taken because I didn't waste time hopping from digging, to
turning on the water hose to planting and back to digging. I
dug all the holes at once, watered them all, and planted. I was
more efficient because I stayed on task. And what helped me
to do that? First, there was lack of water that forced me to do it.
Second, I passed the time by talking with my Heavenly Father.
What normally would have been a mundane task became
something enjoyable.

I've decided that the next time I get tempted to hop from one
thing to the next or when I'm stuck in a situation where I'm
missing a key resource that I need, that I'll stay on task, doing
what I can do, and pass the time consulting with my Heavenly Father!

Treasures Within the Pit

Have you ever felt like life has dealt you such a blow that you're in a deep, dark pit? You struggle for months or even years to understand why you're caught in this pit. Over time you learn to look to the Savior and His light begins to shine in and illuminate the crevices of the pit. You learn to lean on Him and your burden is lightened, but still you long for the fresh air and sunshine that emerging completely from the pit would afford.

You want to walk side by side with your Savior along sandy sunlit beaches, drinking in the blue skies and feeling the breeze on your face. But alas, you're stuck in a pit – trapped by some form of bondage. It may be of your own making or it may simply be one of life's unexplainable blows. Whether it is physical, mental, financial or spiritual, you long to fly, but you're chained inside the pit.

As I was thinking about my own pit, I found myself begging the Lord for fresh air, sunlight and freedom from my own personal trials. Surely I've learned the lessons from them by now? Surely it's time to move on to bluer skies. The words of James Allen in his book *As a Man Thinketh* came to mind, "As the progressive and evolving being, man is where he is that he may learn that he may grow; and as he learns the spiritual lesson which any circumstance contains for him, it passes away and gives place to other circumstances."

As I pondered and prayed about my own situation, the Lord led me to look for the spiritual lessons and treasures within this pit. What were the good things that came from it? I put pen to paper and listed them. As I stood back and asked myself, What would you trade for these treasures? Would you trade $50,000 for them? No. Would you trade a million dollars for them? No. Would you trade all the money in the world for them? The answer would still be No.

At that point, I realized that since I am still in the pit, there must still be treasures here. To ask the Lord to prematurely remove me from the pit would deny me the priceless treasures that are rightly mine. Perhaps I'd even have to descend to the pit at a later time to obtain them. Gratitude filled my heart for the pit and the treasures that it contained. It became easier to be patient with the Lord's timing so that all the treasures can be found.

I enjoy the writings of Isaiah. They have so many levels of meaning. Isaiah 51:1 and 3 in particular holds personal meaning for me and perhaps it will for you. It says, "Hearken unto me, ye that follow after righteousness, ye that seek the Lord; look unto the rock whence ye are hewn and to the hole of the pit whence ye were dug… For the LORD shall comfort Zion: he will comfort all her waste places; and he will make her wilderness like Eden, and her desert like the garden of the Lord; joy and gladness shall be found therein, thanksgiving, and the voice of melody."

As we look to our Rock, our Redeemer, we begin to see that the pit from which we are dug is a blessing in disguise. It molds and shapes us into the person He wants us to be. Life isn't about having or doing. It's about *becoming* who the Lord knows we can be. Within life's hardest challenges and trials lie treasures of knowledge, wisdom, relationships, talents and self-discovery. From now on, I'll be looking at my pit with new eyes. I'll be searching in the Light of Christ for every good thing that can be found here and when I've found all there is in this pit, the Lord is faithful to His promises. He will comfort all my waste places, turn my wilderness into Eden and make my desert like the garden of the Lord. I can gratefully find happiness now as I relax and enjoy the journey, looking for miracles along the way.

A Matter of Perspective

"It may be that the Lord will look on mine affliction, and that
the Lord will requite me good for his cursing this day."
2 Samuel 16:12

In my last study lesson, I wrote about finding treasures within
our own personal pits of pain. Since writing that article, the
Lord led me through an interesting bread trail of lessons to
help me see my "pit" a little differently. The following Saturday afternoon, I walked next door to my sister's house to help
her with a computer problem and on the way home noticed
the gorgeous day. The sky was blue, the weather perfect, and
the landscape beckoning. On a whim, I took off into the field
in front of our houses. My sister's family and ours share
twenty-four acres of beautiful North Georgia landscape, and it
called out to me that afternoon.

I'm ashamed to say that it had probably been ten months
since I'd last taken a stroll like this. As I ventured on, the
realization struck me that I am not in a pit after all. We have
so much abundance, but in my myopic view of things, I'd let
one problem in my life become my world. While I'd seen some
of my treasures, I'd become totally oblivious to a large portion
of my blessings because I'd been focusing so much on one
area of lack. I'd in essence chosen to be in a pit, when I could
have easily ascended to the light of day anytime I wished.
**Lesson 1: Abundance is a choice I can make at any time as
long as I open my eyes to it.**

I strolled back toward the house picking up a pocket-full of scaly bark hickory nuts from those that litter our property. Sitting down on a hay wagon, I began cracking open these hickory nuts with a rock and enjoying the tasty meat within. It became a bit of a game to see if I could hit them just right to retrieve all the meat in the most complete form. I chuckled when I realized that if someone had forced me to perform this labor, it would have felt like a chore. But since it was something I *wanted* to do, it became a relaxing diversion. **Lesson 2: Events just are. Whether we see them as good or bad is primarily in how we look at them. The trick is in finding the good within any task.**

A third piece to this bread trail happened over the next week or so when several people confided their serious challenges to me: one suffering from health problems, another an unfaithful spouse, another family rifts, another family members who've lost their way. When I compare my problem to theirs, I realize that I prefer my challenge to theirs any day. **Lesson 3: Be grateful that you have the trials that are best suited to you.**

In this bread trail of insights, the Lord has been trying to teach me the following principles:

- **Start noticing *all* the blessings you have.** Focus on the good and the bad will minimize.
- **Learn to enjoy the challenges of your life.** Make them a game, experiment, learn to work with them. Let them teach you something and find joy in them.
- **Focus on serving, praying for and helping others and your own problems will fall into perspective.**

Other people have it a lot worse than you do. As the
old saying goes, "I once thought I had it bad because
I had no shoes, until I met a man that had no feet."

Problems and challenges are a part of life. It doesn't matter
your faith or lack of it, you will encounter challenges. As 1
Peter 4:12-13 says, "Beloved, think it not strange concerning
the fiery trial which is to try you, as though some strange
thing happened unto you: But rejoice, inasmuch as ye are
partakers of Christ's sufferings; that, when his glory shall be
revealed, ye may be glad also with exceeding joy."

The consolation is that when we put our trust in the Lord,
look for the good, and express gratitude for the lessons within
our trials, we can find joy and peace even when life is not
perfect. Through the perspective the gospel brings, we learn
that what Jesus promised is true, "Peace I leave with you, my
peace I give unto you: not as the world giveth, give I unto you.
Let not your heart be troubled, neither let it be afraid" (John
14:27) As Paul said, may "the peace of God, which passes all
understanding keep your hearts and minds through Christ
Jesus" (Philippians 4:7).

A Pillar of Fire to Lead the Way

Have you ever felt like you were walking blind through life, not knowing day to day what to do or how to do it? Have you ever wished that the Lord's direction were as constant and visible in your life as the pillar of fire that led the children of Israel? It can be. You don't have to walk blindly. You can have the Holy Spirit as your guide.

Sometimes the light the Holy Spirit brings is abundant and bright, at other times it leads us line upon line and precept upon precept. (Isaiah 28:13) In the wilderness experiences of life, we often feel like the Lord is only giving us direction on a "need to know basis" just as the Israelites were given only enough manna for the day it was gathered (Exodus 16:15-35). Gordon B. Hinckley used the analogy of a locomotive to describe this phenomenon:

"Long ago I worked for one of our railroads. I frequently rode the trains. It was in the days when there were steam locomotives. Those great monsters of the rails were huge and fast and dangerous. I often wondered how the engineer dared the long journey through the night. Then I came to realize that it was not one long journey, but rather a constant continuation of a short journey. The engine had a powerful headlight that made bright the way for a distance of 400 or 500 yards. The engineer saw only that distance, and that was enough, because it was constantly before him all through the night into the dawn of the new day…. And so it is with our eternal journey. We take one step at a time. In doing so we reach toward the unknown, but faith lights the way. If we will cultivate that faith, we shall never walk in darkness." [1]

The children of Israel cultivated faith in their wilderness experience. They spent 40 years learning to trust the Lord and have faith in Him. In the wilderness, they whined and complained for water, and Moses struck rocks to bring forth water for them to drink (Num. 20: 10-11, Exodus 17:6). When they whined for food, the Lord dropped manna from the skies. They were dependent upon others to provide their daily food and water. They didn't have the power or the faith to access inspiration on their own. Contrast this with the Promised Land where an abundant variety of food was readily available and where brooks, fountains and springs came up out of the valleys and hills (See Deuteronomy 8:7-17) Only those who had developed faith and trust could receive the abundant blessings of the Promised Land.

Paul taught the Corinthians that the Rock that Moses struck for water symbolized Jesus Christ – the Rock and foundation of our faith (see 1 Corinthians 10:1-6). And according to the Savior, the manna also represented Him. John 6:31-35 says, "Our fathers did eat manna in the desert; as it is written, He gave them bread from heaven to eat. Verily, verily, I say unto you, Moses gave you not that bread from heaven; but my Father giveth you the true bread from heaven. For the bread of God is he which cometh down from heaven, and giveth life unto the world...I am the bread of life: he that cometh to me shall never hunger; and he that believeth on me shall never thirst."

Just as food and water flows more abundantly in the Promised Land, so does guidance from the Holy Ghost in our spiritual Promised Land. Your goal is to get to and stay in a spiritual Promised Land where the inspiration flows in

abundance. You want to begin to catch a vision of the big
picture and be led by the constant companionship of the Holy
Ghost who confirms each step you make – like that light on
the locomotive leading the way. The closer we live to the
Spirit, the fewer mistakes we make. In time, you learn to listen
to the still small voice. You learn to distinguish the peace and
the comfort the Spirit brings. But it's more than just learning.
The gift of the Holy Ghost is just that - a gift - a constant
companion rather than an occasional visitor. It's the difference between striking the rock to make the water flow out and
being in the Promised Land where the water bubbles up in
abundance from natural springs.

But how do you enter the Promised Land? The children of
Israel needed two important things to enter their Promised
Land. They needed enough faith and trust in God to follow
where He led them, and they needed to make and keep
covenants with the Lord.

Making and Keeping Covenants

A covenant is a two-way promise where we promise the Lord
something and He promises us something in return. For
example, the Abrahamic covenant is the ultimate example
with the result being a Promised Land for Abraham and
Sarah and their posterity. In Genesis 15 & 17 the Lord covenants with Abraham and Sarah (then childless) to give them
a posterity as numerous as the sands of the sea, and gave
them the land of Canaan as the Promised Land for them and
their posterity. This same covenant was renewed with Isaac

(Genesis 26:1-5, 24) and Jacob (Genesis 28:1-4, 10-14; Genesis 35:9-13; Genesis 48:3-4).

Again, the Lord renewed this covenant with the children of Israel at the mountain. The Lord gave Moses the stipulations of the covenant, "Now therefore, if ye will obey my voice indeed, and keep my covenant, then ye shall be a peculiar treasure unto me above all people: for the earth is mine: And ye shall be unto me a kingdom of priests, and an holy nation. These are the words which thou shalt speak unto the children of Israel."

"And Moses came and called for the elders of the people, and laid before their faces all these words which the Lord commanded him. And all the people answered together, and said, All that the Lord hath spoken we will do. And Moses returned the words of the people unto the Lord" (Exodus 19:3-8).

They broke this agreement shortly after when they had Aaron shape the golden calf. Repeatedly they broke this covenant and subsequently lost the guiding and protective power of the Holy Spirit. They did not heed Moses' warning: "Take heed unto yourselves, lest ye forget the covenant of the Lord your God, which he made with you, and make you a graven image, or the likeness of any thing, which the Lord thy God hath forbidden thee" (Deuteronomy 4:23). As long as they kept their part of the covenant, the Lord blessed them. But when they broke their covenant – usually by worshipping idols – they lost these privileges and blessings and eventually were scattered throughout the nations of the earth (See Deuteronomy 31:16-22). The Lord is bound when we do what He says, but when we don't, we have no promise.

Today, I'd say there are very few of us who are going to make golden calves and bow down to them, but we do have our idols. They may be money, pleasure, fame, wealth, sports, TV or even our careers. Jeremiah seems to have been speaking to us directly today when he spoke of those who "worshipped the works of their own hands" (Jeremiah 1:16).

Anything that occupies a higher place in our hearts than God blocks our ability to see, hear and understand the messages from the Holy Spirit. We cannot hear a Master we do not serve. Like the Israelites, if we want to enter and remain in our Promised Land, we must make and keep covenants with Him to keep Him first in our hearts. When we become Christ's, we become "Abraham's seed and heirs according to the promise" (Galatians 3:27-29). We must develop faith and trust that He has our best interests at heart. We must hunger and thirst for the truth and His guidance – Christ's living waters and Bread of Life. It takes opening our minds to the possibilities, and looking beyond the obvious realities – beyond the giants and the walled cities - and seeing the divine possibilities that only God can deliver. Then, and only then, may we hope to enter and remain in our Promised Land.

1)   Gordon B. Hinckley, "We Live By Faith," April 2002

Why Do Bad Things
Happen to Good People?

A lady who had recently suffered a miscarriage wrote me. She
was suffering a great deal of pain and confusion about why
the Lord would let this "evil" come upon her. Why didn't He
protect her and her baby? Why had He let her down? Having
suffered a miscarriage myself, I can understand the emptiness
she's going through, but knowledge of our Heavenly Father
and His plan for us gave me peace not only in that particularly painful situation, but also in every trial I've ever endured.

What is our Heavenly Father's Plan? And how does it bring
peace in trying situations? If we go back to Adam and Eve in
the Garden of Eden and read in Genesis 2 and 3, we see that
Adam and Eve made a choice. They could have stayed in a
perfect environment, never knowing good from evil, pleasure
from pain, nor joy from suffering. In the very day that God
placed Adam and Eve in the Garden, He presented them with
a choice – to stay in the garden or to eat from the Tree of the
Knowledge of Good and Evil. If they stayed in the garden they
would never learn compassion because there would be no
suffering, never learn patience because there would be no
want, never learn faith because they would walk by sight.
They were free to choose, but He warned them that if they ate
of that tree, they would experience death – both spiritual
death (separation from God) and physical death (separation
of the spirit from the body).

We do not know how long Adam and Eve were in the Garden
or how thoroughly they weighed the choices presented to
them, but a choice was made and that choice was a "trans-
gression" or going-across from one plain of existence to
another. Their choice brought spiritual and physical death
into the world. Life became a schoolroom – a place to learn,
grow and experience a full range of emotions, challenges,
adversities, pleasures and joys. They would have to deal with
the pains and sorrow of childbirth, the frustrations of thorns
and thistles. The earth would no longer bring forth fruits and
vegetables spontaneously (Genesis 3:16-19). They would learn
the satisfaction of a hard day's work and the exhilaration of
sowing a seed in faith that one day it will yield its fruit.

Upon entering this schoolroom of mortality they learned that
there is an opposition in all things. Everything is a compound
in one – within every bad situation, there is an equal and
opposite good. To truly understand pleasure, we must endure
pain. To value virtue, one must be exposed to vice. To bask in
the light of faith, we must have traversed the darkness of
doubt. Even the Savior Himself was required to endure a
wilderness experience and temptation before He embarked on
His earthly ministry (Mark 1). The Son of God was no exception to this requirement.

The choice made in the Garden affects all of us to this day. We
live in a fallen world. This schoolroom is a place for us to
learn, grow, and develop in ways we never could in a heavenly or Eden atmosphere. It is a temporary state. It's only a
single act of a play that goes on for eternity. Birth is the
entrance to this schoolroom and death is merely the exit. All is
not lost upon walking through the portal we call death. It is

simply a transition. Death is not the end, because our Heavenly Father in His infinite wisdom prepared a Savior for us. The Bible tells us that Jesus Christ was "foreordained before the foundation of the world" (1 Peter 1:20) as the "Lamb slain from the foundation of the world" (Revelation 13:8). His sacrifice for us was planned from the beginning. God knew the choice that Adam and Eve would make in the Garden. He knew we would enter mortality where we would learn, grow and develop in ways we never could otherwise.

If every time we were to stub our toe, make a mistake or experience pain, an angel came to stop the event, what would we learn from this life? If only the wicked were punished and the good were always blessed, how much faith would be necessary to choose righteously? Jesus taught that our Father in heaven "maketh the sun to rise on the evil and on the good, and sendeth rain on the just and the unjust" (Matthew 5:45). When Job's wife told him to just "curse God and die" he replied, "You speak as the foolish women speak. What? Shall we receive good at the hand of God, and shall we not receive evil?" The Bible tells us that in all his afflictions Job did not "sin with his lips" (Job 2:9-10).

Even in his worst pain, Job trusted the Lord and prophesied, "For I know that my redeemer liveth, and that he shall stand at the latter day upon the earth: and though after my skin worms destroy this body, yet in the flesh shall I see God" (Job 19:25-26). Job knew that "For as in Adam all die, even so in Christ shall all be made alive" (1 Corinthians 15:22).

Death is not the end, it is simply a door. Pain and suffering are the flipside of a coin shared by joy and happiness. It is when we realize that our adversities are our blessings that we begin to look for the lesson and treasure hidden within every trial. Pain, troubles and distress lead to spiritual growth and progress when we turn to the Lord. This is why James told us to "count it all joy when we fall into divers temptations (problems, challenges)" (James 1:2). If something is a little bad, there's a little good laced within it. If it's catastrophic, then something phenomenal will come as a result. Never doubt that God will make "all things work together for your good" (Romans 8:28). But you must look for it. If you concentrate on the lowly squalid and mean, that is all you will find. But if you look for whatsoever is lovely, virtuous, praiseworthy or of good report, you will find those as well (Philippians 4:8).

Jesus said to Martha, "I am the resurrection, and the life: he that believeth in me, though he were dead, yet shall he live" (John 11:25). Jesus Christ overcame physical death for all through His resurrection (1 Corinthians 15:22) and through His sacrifice conquered spiritual death for all those who believe and follow Him. Death is not the end nor is it evil; it is simply a doorway to eternal life. If we must concern ourselves with any form of death, let us do so with spiritual death. Let us never separate ourselves from God from whom all blessings, riches, knowledge and peace flows. Let us put our trust in Him and He will teach us how to find peace no matter what befalls us in this fallen world.

I Will Not Leave
You Comfortless

Lately, I've noticed an inordinate number of women who
come to SheLovesGod who are struggling with depression,
despondency, and self-doubt. I've wondered whether they are
led to the site because they are looking to God for answers or
whether it's just the state of today's world. So few people seem
to really know comfort – the comfort that only God can bring
into our lives. Even those who profess Him seem to be struggling. We might lament today as Jeremiah did, "Is there no
balm in Gilead? Is there no physician there? Why then is not
the health of the daughter of my people recovered?" (Jeremiah
8:22)

Jesus promised, "Peace I leave with you, my peace I give unto
you: not as the world giveth, give I unto you. Let not your
heart be troubled, neither let it be afraid" (John 14:27). But
where is this comfort? Why do so few seem to be able to grasp
and enjoy it? We could blame it on the world and the sad state
of affairs. We live in a world where reverence for God is
considered politically incorrect and foolish and where small
children are exposed to violence and immorality on every
side. But this really is no excuse. For "God, even the Father of
our Lord Jesus Christ, the Father of mercies, and the God of all
comfort; comforteth us in all our tribulation" (2 Corinthians
1:3-4). He comforts us in *all* our tribulation. But why does it
still feel so far away? How do we grasp this comfort of which
the Savior and the prophets speak?

Seek the Spirit

The Holy Ghost is known as the Comforter. "But the Comforter, which is the Holy Ghost, whom the Father will send in my name, he shall teach you all things, and bring all things to your remembrance, whatsoever I have said unto you" (John 14:26). In our most challenging moments, the Holy Ghost can bring scriptures, quotes or memories to our mind that will help us to find comfort. If we actively seek and listen to the Spirit, the Holy Ghost will teach us the things we need to know and do to find solutions to our problems and the strength to endure them with peace of mind.

It was through the power of the Holy Ghost that the churches in Judaea and Galilee and Samaria, were edified; "and walked ... in the comfort of the Holy Ghost" (Acts 9:31).

Have Faith

When the woman with the issue of blood groped through the multitude to touch the hem of the Savior's garment to be healed, the Savior turned around and said, "Daughter, be of good comfort; thy faith hath made thee whole" (Matthew 9:22). Our faith, in large measure, controls the number of blessings we receive. Through faith we activate the powers of heaven and put them to work in our behalf. This woman, through her faith, pulled virtue from the Savior of mankind and enabled herself to be healed through faith in Him.

Come unto Christ

"Come unto me, all ye that labour and are heavy laden, and I will give you rest. Take my yoke upon you, and learn of me; for I am meek and lowly in heart: and ye shall find rest unto your souls. For my yoke is easy, and my burden is light" (Matthew 11:28-30). How do we come unto Christ? We learn about Him! We learn of His characteristics and His attributes. We emulate Him and do our best to walk in His footsteps by following His perfect example. In any dilemma, we might ask ourselves, "What would Jesus do?" and act more courageously upon the answer.

Study the Scriptures

"For whatsoever things were written aforetime were written for our learning, that we through patience and comfort of the scriptures might have hope" (Romans 15:4). The scriptures are a guidebook for happiness in life. They teach us how to live in such a way that we can find happiness and comfort. When we keep the commandments, we find safety and peace. When we violate heavenly laws, we risk the consequences that come from breaking those laws. If we try to defy gravity and walk off the edge of a precipice, we will suffer the consequences of attempting to break that law. Similarly, the Lord educates us about divine laws in His scriptures. If we wish to have safety and peace, we must learn these divine laws and live in accordance with them.

Patricia R. Holland compared "meeting God in the scriptures" to "a divine intravenous feeding."[1] Are you feeding your spirit every day? Or is it starving?

Keep the Commandments

Christ himself comes to and manifests Himself to those who love Him and keep His commandments. In John 14:18,21 He says, "I will not leave you comfortless: I will come to you…He that hath my commandments, and keepeth them, he it is that loveth me: and he that loveth me shall be loved of my Father, and I will love him, and will manifest myself to him." We might ask ourselves, "Do I do my best to keep the commandments of God? Is it the desire of my heart? Am I daily repenting, learning and trying to more fully live according to His will?"

Repent and Help Others Repent

Paul wrote that he and those who were with him had no rest when they first arrived in Macedonia. They "were troubled on every side; without were fightings, within were fears." Sounds a lot like the world we live in today. But still Paul declares, "I am filled with comfort, I am exceeding joyful in all our tribulation." What brought this joyfulness amidst so much tribulation? It was the joy he found in hearing that the saints had repented. He had been bold with them and thought that perhaps they might be offended with his words, but instead they were filled with godly sorry that worked repentance, change and carefulness in them. (See 2 Corinthians 7:4-10.)

Repentance brings peace. And when we act as instruments in God's hands to lead others to repentance, we find comfort and joy that cannot be matched in any other way. Even when we are faced with our own problems and worries, they somehow

lighten on our backs as we find joy and rejoicing in the
repentance and salvation of another.

Reach Beyond Yourself

God "*comforts* us in all our tribulation, that we may be able to
comfort them which are in any trouble" 2 Corinthians 1:3-4.
We are His messengers, His angels, to deliver comfort to those
who are in need. It is our job as Disciples of Christ to "comfort
each other, edify each other" – with patience toward all. We
are to "comfort the feebleminded and supporting the weak"
(See Thessalonians 5:11,14).

It has been said that "the errand of angels is given to women"
and perhaps this is because by our natures women have a
tendency toward feelings of charity and are inclined to
nurture and comfort. When you utilize your God-given talents
to comfort those that stand in need of comfort, you are acting
as His angel. You are performing His work, "for inasmuch as
ye have done it unto one of the least of these my *sister* ye have
done it unto me" (Matthew 25:40).

1) Patricia Holland, *Many Things... One Thing,* BYU
    Women's Conference 2000, Provo, UT

Decision-Making with Confidence

I was talking to a friend recently who was weighing a difficult business decision. She explained, "I have a tough time making decisions. I labor over them — weighing their pros and cons, but then I'm never really sure which decision is right or whether the decision I finally make is the best one. Heck, I can't even select the toppings for my pizza!"

This is a common problem for a lot of us. Some people can make decisions quickly and move on, while others take lots of time making a decision and then still aren't sure whether the choice they have made is the right one. Does it really have to take this long? Do we really have to walk blindly — never knowing if the choice we made was really the best one?

No! We can make informed decisions and walk forward in faith that our course is the right one. But, we have to lean on Him who knows the end from the beginning. He knows which path is right. He knows which course will lead us to the most happiness. As Proverbs 3:4-6 advises: "Trust in the LORD with all thine heart; and lean not unto thine own understanding. In all thy ways acknowledge him, and he shall direct thy paths."

This is not to say that God is going to give you the answer for every frivolous decision in your life like which outfit to wear today, or what topping to have on your pizza. But on important issues that affect your life, the Lord is willing and waiting for you to ask his opinion.

But, he isn't going to just give you the answer either. God gave us our minds for a reason. He wants us to use them. In Luke 14:28-30, Jesus suggests we weigh the consequences of our actions, "For which of you, intending to build a tower, sitteth not down first, and counteth the cost, whether he have sufficient to finish it? Lest haply, after he hath laid the foundation, and is not able to finish it, all that behold it begin to mock him, Saying, This man began to build, and was not able to finish." Study the pros and cons of any question in your own mind. Use your own logic; pay attention to any feelings or warning signals you may experience. If you have to, write these pros and cons down on paper. Come to your own decision.

Then, go to the Lord in prayer and tell him what you have decided to do, and ask him if it is the right thing to do. As James 1:5-8 admonishes, "If any of you lack wisdom, let him ask of God, that giveth to all men liberally, and upbraideth not; and it shall be given him. But let him ask in faith, nothing wavering. For he that wavereth is like a wave of the sea driven with the wind and tossed. For let not that man think that he shall receive any thing of the Lord. A double minded man is unstable in all his ways."

Notice that James teaches that God is willing to give us wisdom and help when we ask him. But we have to ask in faith, nothing wavering. We can't be wish-washy, indecisive and tossed. Generally speaking, we should come to our own decision, then ask God if it is right. He doesn't like double mindedness. It's easier for us to get a clearer message from our prayers if we've put the thought and study into it and then go to him for a Yes or No answer. Ask God to give you a feeling of peace if it is correct or a bad feeling if it is the wrong choice.

After you pray, listen closely for any feelings you may have. If you have feelings of peace, excitement, happiness or joy afterwards, then you know you've made the correct decision. If you feel depressed, unsure, uneasy or disturbed, you know it's not the right decision. Go back to the drawing board and start again.

There are some times in your life when you'll make a decision and pray about it and feel nothing either way. Some decisions may not matter all that much in your life or in the eternal scheme of things. Either decision may be just fine. In these cases, the Lord will leave that choice up to you.

The Lord is there for you. He has told us to ask and we shall receive, seek and we shall find, knock and it shall be opened unto us. Don't lean on your own understanding when a confirmation of your decisions is so easy to obtain. Ask God in faith, nothing wavering and you can go forward in confidence that your choices are right.

Is It God or Is It Just My Imagination?

Jesus explained that some people are so blind in their eyes and hardened in their hearts that they will not see with their eyes nor understand with their hearts and be converted, that "I should heal them" (John 12:40). Notice the word heal in this verse. He's talking about more than physical healing here. He's talking about spiritual healing as well. Think of the spiritual bruises and wounds we suffer – sometimes through our own poor choices or from the mistakes and maliciousness of others. Jesus is saying if we will open our eyes, soften our hearts and allow ourselves to understand His message until we are converted, He will heal us. That's quite a promise!

Those who will not hear, see or open their hearts refuse His healing touch. Christ never forces Himself upon us. He never takes away our freedom of choice – even if it's for "our own good." This is important to remember as we speak with those who are struggling in their faith or who have their eyes closed and their hearts hardened. We should never seek to force, coerce or berate someone into believing or living a Christ-like life. Rather, we should love and serve them and give them time to adjust their eyes to the light.

Jesus often taught through parables. He did this because each individual in His audience was at a different level of hearing and understanding. Some could comprehend the deeper mysteries while others were having a tough time with the basics. Still others were completely hardened and blind. It was a benevolent thing for Him to teach in parables for "unto whom much is given, much is required" (Luke 12:48). Parables allowed people to hear and understand as much as they were able to handle without giving them too much for which to be accountable.

In John 16 Jesus explains to His disciples in a proverbial way that He will go away from them and they won't see Him and then He will come back. They began consulting with each other trying to figure out what He was talking about. They were confused and really wanted Him to speak plainly to them. But no one asked Him point-blank what He meant.

Then Jesus, knowing that they wanted to ask Him but wouldn't, said "Do ye inquire among yourselves what I said, A little while and ye shall not see me: and again a little while, and ye shall see me?" Then He explained that He would be taken from them and they would weep and sorrow for the loss, but He would return again and they would have great joy that no man could take from them.

He then admonished, "Hitherto have ye asked nothing in my name: ask, and ye shall receive, that your joy may be full. These things have I spoken unto you in proverbs: but the time cometh, when I shall no more speak unto you in proverbs, but I shall show you plainly of the Father. At that day ye shall ask in my name…" (John 16:24-26)

After this plainer explanation His disciples rejoiced, "Lo, now speakest thou plainly, and speakest no proverb. Now are we sure that thou knowest all things … by this we believe that thou camest forth from God" (John 16:29-30).

Notice what Jesus is teaching them here. When they couldn't understand His initial teaching, they were either too proud or ashamed to admit they didn't understand. So they just asked each other. Jesus proved to them that He knew their thoughts – that He knows all things by going ahead and answering a question that they were too proud or afraid to ask. Then He told them in essence, "Ask. If you want to understand something that is unclear, just ask the Father in my name and you'll have your answer."

While conversing with others can be beneficial, sometimes we lean too heavily on other people for answers and forget to ask our Heavenly Father in the name of His Son Jesus Christ for the answer we need. If you are unclear, ask Him! But what if you ask but are unsure whether the answer you receive is from God or just your own thoughts or desires?

On November 16, 2002, I went to hear one of my favorite speakers/authors, Sheri Dew address a group of women in Asheville, NC. She remarked that many years ago when she was less educated in the language of the Spirit, she asked a mentor friend, "What if I can't tell the difference between the voice of the Lord and my own thinking?" The friend asked, "Have you asked the Lord to teach you how to tell the difference?" She admitted she hadn't. So she began praying and asking, "Teach me what it sounds like/feels like when you speak to me." In time through immersing herself in the scriptures, she learned to distinguish the voice of the Lord from her own thoughts. She compared learning the language of the Spirit to learning any other language. We have to become familiar with the rules, grammar, and vocabulary. We learn these in the scriptures. God's Word teaches us what we can do to bring the Spirit closer and what drives it away. She said, "I have found over the years that the Spirit comes more clearly and more often when I immerse myself in the scriptures."

In John 14:26-27 Jesus promised, "But the Comforter, which is the Holy Ghost, whom the Father will send in my name, he shall teach you all things, and bring all things to your remembrance, whatsoever I have said unto you. Peace I leave with you, my peace I give unto you: not as the world giveth, give I unto you. Let not your heart be troubled, neither let it be afraid."

I think the greatest disservice we do to ourselves is forgetting or questioning the peace that the Spirit brings when we pray and get an answer. If we study, ponder and pray about something and we get a feeling of peace about it, in time we tend to question whether we really got an answer. Satan loves to shake our confidence and tell us that we are just fooling ourselves. But Jesus taught that the Comforter speaks peace to our hearts and He brings all things to our remembrance – whatever the Lord has said to us. If we seek to live in harmony with the teachings of Jesus and seek to purify our lives through Christ, the Spirit will become stronger in our lives. The Spirit will help us remember the night we cried to the Lord and He spoke peace to our souls concerning the matter.

Then, when others question our actions or when opposition strikes, we can rest assured that the Lord gave us the answer when we prayed, and we can hold out in faith without fear or doubt knowing that there is a perfect time for all good things to come to fruition. Jesus said, "In the world ye shall have tribulation: but be of good cheer; I have overcome the world" (John 16:33). When we pray and receive an answer on anything of importance – on anything that will do some good in the world – Satan immediately attacks to shake our confidence. Don't let Him. Cast your mind back on the time when you prayed and received your answer. Lean on that. Don't question it. Walk on in faith and "cast not away your confidence, which hath great recompence of reward" (Hebrews 10:35).

Why Aren't My Prayers Being Answered?

Recently I've had several people write to say that although they do their best to have faith in the Lord and to follow His teachings, they do not receive answers to their prayers. It is as if they are praying to the ceiling, for it seems they are neither heard nor answered.

How can this be, when the scriptures continually remind us to "ask and ye shall receive; knock and it shall be opened unto you"? The Lord does not lie, so there must be something else at work here. Perhaps we do not understand how our prayers are being answered. Perhaps we do not recognize the answers when they come, or maybe some other factor is at work.

How desperate are you?

Often when our need is most desperate, answers seem slowest in coming. Have you ever been in a hurry to get out the door but can't find your keys? You're desperate — you search everywhere with no luck. Then you decide to sit for a minute and calm down and think. You get up and there your keys are, in an obvious location that you may have even searched before. Similarly, in our frantic state, we are often too stressed to open our spiritual eyes and see answers that are in plain view. Sometimes our cries for help drown out the still small voice that is speaking the answers.

Relax. Try to emotionally detach yourself from the situation, look at it objectively, find a quiet place to pray and really listen for answers.

Do You Already Have the Answer?

Sometimes we pray for things that we already know the answer to. Within the scriptures are advice and direction in the way that we should live. Have you searched the scriptures for your answer? For example, if you are struggling with whether you should forgive a person who has seriously offended you, and you pray to the Lord for guidance in this, you may feel you aren't getting an answer. But in reality, the answer has already been given to you. It is found in the scriptures. (See Matthew 18:21-35)

Sometimes we think that we're the exception to the rule. "Sure, I know the scriptures teach that, but my case is different. I need the Lord to tell me specifically what to do in my situation." But the truth is you and I are NOT the exceptions. We need to be willing to act upon the Lord's commands first. Then, as we act, we will feel a confirmation that our decision is the right one. We will have feelings of peace and contentment that following the Lord's commandments is truly the best course for us. But, it is up to us to **act before** we get an answer in such cases. "If any man will **do** his will, he shall know of the doctrine, whether it be of God, or whether I speak of myself" (John 7:17).

He Never Promised A "Yes"

Because the Lord has an eternal perspective on our existence, He knows best about what we need in our lives. Sometimes, in our own best interests, the Lord tells us "No" – even when we pray for something that seems like it should be perfectly acceptable in His sight. It takes faith to believe that Heavenly Father knows best and that if He says "No" that that's still an answer, and it's one that will be best for us in the long run.

He Never Promised "When"

The Lord often asks us to wait a while. His timing is always the best timing. "Since faith in the timing of the Lord may be tried, let us learn to say not only, 'Thy will be done,' but patiently also, 'Thy timing be done.'" [1] I am reminded of a tough six years in our married life when my husband and I experienced serious financial challenges. The answer to our prayers was not that we would be immediately delivered from our financial situation, instead we were given hope, peace and the ability to endure it as we worked to correct the situation. The Lord often wants us to work through serious challenges so that we can grow in wisdom and faith. In such cases, I have found it helpful to ask, "What can I learn from this situation? What do I know now and how am I a better person for having endured this hardship?" I have found that the lessons learned are always worth the price paid.

He Will Not Force the Agency of Others

I have learned that although we may have faith in the Lord
and what He would like to have happen, we can't always
count on other people to use their free will (agency) to choose
what the Lord wants. When our prayers involve the choices of
others, we must be especially patient. The Lord will never
force anyone to see the light or to choose His will in answer to
your prayers. He may gently persuade, lead and guide them
until they eventually see the light, but He will not force
Himself upon them. Patience is critical when our prayers
involve the agency of others.

Did You Hear That Answer?

Moses heard the Lord's voice from a burning bush. Joseph
dreamed dreams. Saul (later Paul) saw a vision, but rarely do
we hear voices, see visions or dream dreams. Instead, we may
have strokes of ideas or inspiration come into our minds. We
may be reading a verse of scripture and it may trigger ideas for
what we should do next. We may be speaking with a friend
and she may have the answer we seek. Still other times we
may experience a feeling of peace and comfort that lets us
know what we should do. It is important to learn to listen and
recognize answers and not to dismiss them as simply coinci-
dence or our own voice within our head.

There are other factors that can play a role in whether our
prayers are being answered, but they are always on our end of
the communication channel. The Lord always listens. It is up
to us to keep the channels clean by being obedient to the Lord,

listening, learning to recognize His voice, and being willing to accept His will instead of our own.

"If you seek His help, be sure your life is clean, your motives are worthy, and you're willing to do what He asks — for He *will* answer your prayers. He is your loving Father; you are His beloved child. He loves you perfectly and wants to help you." [2]

1)   Neal A. Maxwell, *"Plow in Hope,"* Ensign, May 2001.
2)   Richard G. Scott, *Learning to Recognize Answers to Prayer*, Ensign, November 1989.

How Do You Really Give It to God?

"Give it to God" a friend might advise in your trying circumstance. Good advice, but what does this mean exactly? For
most of us, we muster all our faith to believe that everything
will work out in the end, but struggle daily – giving our
problems to the Lord one day and taking them back the next.
We're like a gardener who plants a seed and worryingly digs
it up to see how the roots are growing – doing more damage
than good.

For years I've struggled with the location of the line between
what I should control and what the Lord controls. How much
am I supposed to do? How little? And how do I muster the
faith to consistently "give it to God" and not worry? Perhaps
you've asked yourself these same questions.

Recently, as He has done on countless occasions, the Lord
brought someone into my life to teach me what I needed to
learn next. There's an old saying, "when the student is ready,
the teacher arrives." This teacher helped me gain a better
understanding of God's laws and how by living in harmony
with them, I could clearly see the line between what I am
supposed to handle and what God will handle. After learning
these laws, I no longer struggle on a day-by-day basis to
muster the faith to "give it to God." I have an unwavering
assurance that enables me to **not only trust the Lord, but also
trust that I will like where He's taking me**. What a sense of
peace! Before this, I thought I had faith, but I don't think I even

scratched the surface of understanding what that word really means.

There's no way to convey all these principles in one article, but my goal is to give you the basics. For more information on this subject visit www.ThoughtsAlive.com.

First let's look at Hebrews 6:10-19. Paul's writings are a little tricky to understand, but there are some key principles in this passage that can help us understand how God works. I compared several translations of this passage, and the Word English Bible seems the plainest:

"For God is not unrighteous, so as to forget your work and the labor of love which you showed toward his name, in that you served the saints, and still do serve them."

In other words, the Lord is mindful of you. He sees how you have worked and labored with love to serve others. He sees that your heart is in the right place and that you are seeking first the Kingdom of God.

"We desire that each one of you may show the same diligence to the fullness of hope even to the end, that you won't be sluggish, but imitators of those who through faith and patience inherited the promises. "

Paul desires that we would through our own diligence have a fullness of hope – all the way to the end. Michael C. Muhammad said, "Everything works out right in the end. If things are not working right, it isn't the end yet. Don't let it bother you, relax and keep on going." When we "give it to God" it doesn't necessarily mean we put everything on hold. We continue to labor and serve others. We continue in the work we can do. The Lord works through our current circumstances to manifest His will. Giving it to God doesn't mean we become lazy and do nothing. Instead, we should be diligent, patient and with an eye of faith work in hope knowing the end will bring the promise.

For when God made a promise to Abraham, since He could swear by none greater, He swore by Himself, saying, "Most surely I will bless you, and I will surely multiply you." Thus, having patiently endured, he obtained the promise.

The Lord promised to multiply Abraham and make him a great nation. But Abraham and Sarah didn't even have their first child together until they were in their 90's! How's that for patience? Abraham patiently endured, kept his covenant with the Lord and obtained the promise. When the Lord promises, He delivers! It may not be on our timetable, but He always delivers in His perfect timing.

"For men indeed swear by a greater one, and in every dispute of theirs the oath is final for confirmation. Wherein God, being determined to show more abundantly to the heirs of the promise the immutability of his counsel, interposed with an oath; that by two immutable things, in which it is impossible for God to lie, we may have a strong encouragement, who have fled for refuge to take hold of the hope set before us, which we have as an anchor of the soul, a hope both sure and steadfast and entering into that which is within the veil;"

When the Lord promises, He always delivers. And most of the time, He makes promises in the form of covenants – two way promises. We promise Him something (our faithfulness) and He promises us something (His blessings). This is what the Abrahamic Covenant was. And when the Lord promises, there's no more need for worry. Our faith becomes hope that acts as an anchor to the soul. It gives us an assurance and a vision of things to come. The term "within the veil" implies those things which are spiritual, beyond this life, or things of a heavenly nature. Our faith almost becomes "other worldly" as we put these principles into practice. We see with our spiritual eyes the things that are currently only spiritual but are moving toward us into physical form.

The best analogy I've heard for this is an acorn. Does an acorn have an oak tree inside of it? It has the plan for an oak tree – right? It doesn't have everything yet, but it has the blueprint or the promise of an oak tree inside of it. If you hold that acorn in your hand long enough will it grow or disintegrate? It will eventually disintegrate – right? If you want it to grow, you have to plant it in the right kind of soil. Then in time, the acorn will become an oak tree.

Does the acorn have to fight and claw to become an oak tree? No, it simply holds the blueprint of the tree in its cell structure and everything that it needs to become a tree is drawn to it out of the soil, air and water. In the appointed gestation period, the acorn becomes a tree.

Similarly, when we have the vision of a goal that the Lord has promised us, we can plant it in our minds, hold the vision of it in faithful diligence with patience for the timing of the Lord.

Diligence with your vision means you act on every prompting that you receive from the Spirit as you hold this vision. No matter how insignificant or silly it may seem, heed the promptings you receive from the Spirit and act immediately on them. From small and simple things are great things brought to pass.

In summary, here are the steps for knowing how to give things to God:

1. **Make sure your heart is in the right place**. Make sure your first and foremost desire is to "seek first the Kingdom of God." For as 1 John 3:19-24 says, "Hereby we know that we are of the truth, and shall assure our hearts before Him. For if our heart condemn us not, then have we confidence toward God. And whatsoever we ask, we receive of Him, because we keep His commandments, and do those things that are pleasing in His sight." If you're living in harmony with the Lord's commands and have His Spirit with you, you won't ask for anything that is contrary to His will. If you do, you'll quickly know it. Whatever your desire, check it against scripture to see if it is a valid request and then ask the Lord for a confirmation that your desire is one that is in harmony with His will.

2. **Once you have His confirmation, you have His promise.** Start with the end in mind. Create a clear vision of what you want in your mind and hold it there, in faith, believing that you will receive it. At this point you are seeing "within the veil." You are in essence seeing the spiritual birth of your promise and eventually through your faith and diligence it will grow into physical form.

3.   **Spend time each day visualizing your outcome that the Lord has promised you.** Visualize it as if it is already yours, because it *is* on its way to you! Be grateful for that! Thank the Lord and praise Him that it is on its way.

4.   **As the Spirit prompts you to do things throughout your day, act immediately.** Act on every burst of insight or prompting from the Spirit. (Note this is assuming you are living God's commands and are worthy of His Spirit. As John 3:24 says, "He that keepeth His commandments dwelleth in Him and He in him. And hereby we know that He abideth in us, by the Spirit which He hath given us." If you aren't living in accordance with God's commands, you can't be certain of the source of impulses.)

5.   **Be patient and diligent, and you *will* attain your goal.** God cannot lie. The Lord is bound when we do what He says. If we don't do what He says, we have no promise. But if you live by His laws and keep your end of the bargain, you will obtain the promise in His perfect timing.

The question for us to ponder is no longer *how* or *if* we will receive the promised blessing; it is simply a matter of *when*. Knowing with this level of assurance that you will receive the promise gives you an amazing level of patience to wait for God's perfect timing. Most importantly, you learn to listen to and trust the Spirit. Ultimately God is in control of everything! You just hold the vision and follow instructions. Like the acorn, there is no need to fight, manipulate or force the outcome. You simply trust the Lord to let things flow and respond when prompted.

The Atonement Is For Victims Too

Have you ever been betrayed by someone you love? Falsely condemned? Unjustly treated? Or perhaps you have been the victim of a crime? We often think of the Atonement as being only for sinners, but the Atonement of Jesus Christ is equally effective in healing the victim. Psalms 147:3 teaches us that Christ "healeth the broken in heart, and bindeth up their wounds."

As an introduction of the purpose of His mortal ministry to the world, Jesus read Isaiah 61:1-4 in the synagogue:

"The Spirit of the Lord GOD is upon me; because the Lord hath anointed me to preach good tidings unto the meek; he hath sent me to bind up the brokenhearted, to proclaim liberty to the captives, and the opening of the prison to them that are bound; To proclaim the acceptable year of the LORD, and the day of vengeance of our God; to comfort all that mourn; To appoint unto them that mourn in Zion, to give unto them beauty for ashes, the oil of joy for mourning, the garment of praise for the spirit of heaviness…"

Isaiah 53:3-5 teaches us that along with being wounded for our transgressions and bruised for our iniquities, Jesus also "hath borne our griefs, and carried our sorrows." Because of this, "with his stripes we are healed" – healed from not only the consequences of our repented sins, but also healed from the wounds of others.

James E Faust said, "The Atonement not only benefits the sinner but also benefits those sinned against—that is, the victims. By forgiving "those who trespass against us" (Matthew 6:13) the Atonement brings a measure of peace and comfort to those who have been innocently victimized by the sins of others. The basic source for the healing of the soul is the Atonement of Jesus Christ. This is true whether it be from the pain of a personal tragedy or a terrible national calamity such as we have recently experienced in New York and Washington, D.C., and near Pittsburgh."[1]

A woman who had been through a painful divorce wrote of her experience in drawing on the healing powers of the Atonement. She said: "Our divorce … did not release me from the obligation to forgive. I truly wanted to do it, but it was as if I had been commanded to do something of which I was simply incapable." Her bishop gave her some sound advice: "Keep a place in your heart for forgiveness, and when it comes, welcome it in." Many months passed as she continued to struggle to forgive. She wrote, "During those long, prayerful moments … I tapped into a life-giving source of comfort from my loving Heavenly Father. I sensed that he was not standing by glaring at me for not having accomplished forgiveness yet; rather he was sorrowing with me as I wept...

"In the final analysis, what happened in my heart is for me an amazing and miraculous evidence of the Atonement of Christ. I had always viewed the Atonement as a means of making repentance work for the sinner. I had not realized that it also makes it possible for the one sinned against to receive into his or her heart the sweet peace of forgiving." [2]

In Matthew 6:14-15 Jesus taught, "For if ye forgive men their trespasses, your heavenly Father will also forgive you: But if ye forgive not men their trespasses, neither will your Father forgive your trespasses." But Jesus does not leave us alone to find this forgiveness. Through a prayerful heart and an earnest desire to forgive, Jesus Christ will give us the strength and peace to forgive. It is important to realize that finding a way to forgive is not really for the benefit of the offender. Rather, it is for the victim. Richard G. Scott said, "Forgiveness … allows the love of God to purge your heart and mind of the poison of hate. It cleanses your consciousness of the desire for revenge. It makes place for the purifying, healing, restoring love of the Lord."[3] An unforgiving heart binds you down. It fetters your soul with depression, despondency, and bitterness. Your soul can never be fully free until you forgive.

This principle is illustrated in the following true story, "During World War II there were terrible examples of man's inhumanity to man. After the war was over and the concentration camps were opened, there was much hatred among the weak and emaciated survivors. In one camp, observers noticed a native of Poland who seemed so robust and peaceful they thought he must have only recently been imprisoned. They were surprised to learn that he had been there over six years! Then, they reasoned, he must not have suffered the terrible atrocities to his family members that most of the prisoners had. But in questioning him, they learned how soldiers had come to his city, lined up against a wall his wife, two daughters, and three small sons, then opened fire with a machine gun. Though he begged to die with them, he had been kept alive because of his knowledge and ability in language translation.

"This Polish father said: 'I had to decide right then ... whether to let myself hate the soldiers who had done this. It was an easy decision, really. I was a lawyer. In my practice I had seen ... what hate could do to people's minds and bodies. Hate had just killed the six people who mattered most to me in the world. I decided then that I would spend the rest of my life — whether it was a few days or many years — loving every person I came in contact with.' [4]

Forgiving others does not mean that we approve of their wrongdoing. It means we cease to dwell on the offense and feel peace. Forgiving someone enables our hearts to be cleansed from anger and hatred toward the offender. This process is not quick nor is it easy, but Heavenly Father will help us as we try to forgive.

"There is no peace in harboring old grudges. There is no peace in reflecting on the pain of old wounds. There is peace only in repentance and forgiveness. This is the sweet peace of the Christ, who said, 'Blessed are the peacemakers; for they shall be called the children of God' (Matthew 5:9)." [5]

There is no better example of forgiving others and finding peace and ultimate joy than in the life of the Savior Himself. "All his life he had been the victim of ugliness. As a newborn infant he had been spirited away to save His life at the instruction of an angel in a dream. ... At the end of a hectic life He had stood in quiet, restrained, divine dignity.

"He was beaten, officially scourged. He wore a crown of thorns. ... He was mocked and jeered. He suffered every indignity at the hands of his own people. ... He was required to carry his own cross. … Finally, with the soldiers and his accusers down below him, he looked upon the Roman soldiers and said these immortal words: *'Father, forgive them; for they know not what they do.'* (Luke 23:34)" [6]

"The injured should do what they can to work through their trials, and the Savior will succor his people according to their infirmities. He will help us carry our burdens. Some injuries are so hurtful and deep that they cannot be healed without help from a higher power and hope for perfect justice and restitution in the hereafter. Since the Savior has suffered anything and everything that we could ever feel or experience, He can help the weak to become stronger. He has personally experienced all of it. He understands our pain and will walk with us even in our darkest hours." [7]

My challenge for each of us is to assess any areas where we have been unforgiving and work toward and pray for the ability to forgive others. As we do this, I know that the Savior, in time, will heal our broken hearts and give us peace.

1)   James E. Faust, "The Atonement: Our Greatest Hope," *Ensign*, Nov. 2001, 18

2)   Name Withheld, "My Journey to Forgiving," *Ensign*, Feb. 1997, 42-43.

3)   Richard G. Scott, *Ensign*, May 1992, 33

4)   George G. Ritchie with Elizabeth Sherrill, *Return from Tomorrow* [Waco, Texas: Chosen Books, 1978], p. 116"

5)   Gordon B. Hinckley *Ensign*, November 1980, 63).

6)   Spencer W. Kimball, *The Miracle of Forgiveness* [1969], 279-80.

7)   James E. Faust, "The Atonement: Our Greatest Hope," *Ensign*, Nov. 2001, 18

Bridge Building: Tangible Expressions of Gratitude

This morning, I went to my computer and logged on to check my email. The very first one I opened was from a dear friend with a message of thanks for our friendship. It made my morning, I'll tell you that! My heart was immediately drawn out to my friend and I felt connected to her as if I were nine hundred miles away spending Thanksgiving with her.

Gratitude is a powerful emotion that draws us closer not only to one another but also to our Father in heaven. In nothing is the Lord more offended than when we refuse to acknowledge His hand in all things, nor is there anything that draws us closer to Him than deep and heartfelt gratitude. James 4:8 tells us to "Draw nigh to God, and he will draw nigh to you."

If you want to feel grateful, then the first step is *remembering*. Moses repeatedly advised the children of Israel to *remember* their days of captivity and their deliverance at the Red Sea. As long as they remembered and were grateful for their deliverance, they remained close to the Lord, protected and comforted. But the moment they began to forget their liberation, they forgot the Lord and made foolish mistakes which led them into dangerous paths of destruction.

Like the children of Israel, we must remember our own personal days of bondage and how the Lord has freed us from them. We must remember our own Red Seas and be grateful. In gratitude, not only is there safety and abundance, but also

there is happiness, freedom and peace. You can't be worried
and grateful at the same time. Nor can you be miserable and
grateful simultaneously. Gratitude is an amazing emotion
that eliminates what one of my favorite religion professors
referred to as the "four D's of the Devil": Despair, Discourage-
ment, Despondency and Doubt.

Gratitude leads us to reach out to others and share the love we
feel in our hearts. In the Levitical law, the Lord laid out a
beautiful principle that I believe we'd do well to practice even
today. To me it is the most profound expression of our gratitude for it transforms that blessed emotion into action,
changing lives for the better.

"But thou shalt remember that thou wast a bondman in Egypt,
and the LORD thy God redeemed thee thence: therefore I
command thee to do this thing. When thou cuttest down thine
harvest in thy field, and hast forgot a sheaf in the field, thou
shalt not go again to fetch it: it shall be for the stranger, for the
fatherless, and for the widow: that the Lord thy God may bless
thee in all the work of thine hands. When thou beatest thine
olive tree, thou shalt not go over the boughs again: it shall be
for the stranger, for the fatherless, and for the widow. When
thou gatherest the grapes of thy vineyard, thou shalt not glean
it afterward: it shall be for the stranger, for the fatherless, and
for the widow. And thou shalt remember that thou wast a
bondman in the land of Egypt: therefore I command thee to do
this thing" (Deuteronomy 24:18-22).

While the majority of us are not farmers today with gleaners
in our fields, the principle of remembering our own bondage

and then sharing with others who are going through what we've been through is the epitome of living the Golden Rule. Who better to lift and bless those who are suffering, than she who has suffered and intimately knows the same emotions, heartache and pain of the sufferer? Having lived through your own bondage and Red Sea, you can then turn around and help those who must cross the same bridge you have crossed.

One of my favorite poems is entitled *The Bridge Builder* by Will Allen Dromgoole. It too suggests that we complete the cycle of gratitude by reaching back and lifting our fellow travelers.

An old man, going a lone highway,
Came at the evening, cold and gray,
To a chasm vast and deep and wide.

The old man crossed in the twilight dim,
The sullen stream had no fear for him;
But he turned when safe on the other side,
And built a bridge to span the tide.

"Old Man", said a fellow pilgrim near,
"You are wasting your strength with building here;
Your journey will end with the ending day,
You never again will pass this way.

You've crossed the chasm deep and wide;
Why build you this bridge at evening tide?"
The builder lifted his old gray head-

"Good friend, in the path I have come",
he said, "There followeth after me today,

A youth whose feet must pass this way;
This chasm that has naught to me
To that fair-haired youth may a pitfall be:
He, too, must cross in the twighlight dim -
Good friend, I am building this bridge for him."

As I look back over this year, I am grateful for those who built
the bridges that I've crossed. I have seen my own Red Seas
part this year, and every one of them has been because the
Lord led people into my life who were kind enough to build a
bridge for me. I am grateful for these people who reach out
and bless others – sometimes without even realizing who will
cross the bridge they leave behind. Some of them intentionally,
selflessly build bridges while others are like the honey bee
who goes about its business doing its work of gathering
nectar, never knowing that it is pollinating a landscape and
making it possible for others to eat.

I am grateful for those who simply do their best in their own
field of endeavor and thus pollinate the world in the process.
And I am immensely thankful for those kind-hearted souls
who intentionally reach out and leave a legacy behind. This
Thanksgiving, let's think about the impact we make on the
world, the bridges we build. Is the world a better place
because we're here? Are we showing the Lord how grateful
we are for all He has done for us by reaching out and sharing
His love with others?

The Key That Unlocks the Treasury of Heaven

There's an old Hasidic story that tells of a man who met two of his friends while traveling down a road. He asked the two men how thing were going in their lives. The first friend answered that things were horrible. He declared that he'd be better off dead. Life was hard and nothing seemed to be going his way. God, hearing their conversation from heaven commented, "You think you've got it bad now, you ungrateful man, you haven't seen anything yet!"

The second friend answered, "Life is wonderful! God is good. Everything is coming up roses. I am so incredibly blessed!" God, hearing this reply from heaven answered, "What a delightfully grateful soul! You think you've got it good now, just wait and see what wonderful things await you!"

The Lord delights to bless those with a grateful heart. Colossians 3:17 gives the secret for making the best of your life: "And whatsoever ye do in word or deed, do all in the name of the Lord Jesus, giving thanks to God and the Father by Him."

Think about that! What if everything you did, you did in the name of the Lord and gave thanks to God in His name! We'd all get into a lot less trouble if we followed this advice wouldn't we? Imagine the good we could do in the world if we took the time to put our best efforts into every task –

knowing that we wanted the Lord Jesus Christ to lend His
name and approval to our every action!

James 4:8 teaches "Draw nigh to God, and He will draw nigh
to you." We draw nigh to God by living His teachings, by
seeking to do what He would have us do, and by showing a
grateful heart. No matter how bad life gets, we can always
find something for which to be grateful. Even in our times of
trouble, we can be thankful knowing that this too shall pass
and the sun will come out tomorrow.

The surest way to bring yourself into harmony with God and
put yourself into a position to receive blessings and directions
at His hand is through a sense of deep and profound gratitude. Gratitude brings you into harmony with the mind and
will of God. It draws you nigh to Him and He in turn will be
drawn to you. Think of it from your own human perspective.
Who are you drawn to more – a person who is ungrateful and
demanding or someone who shows genuine gratitude for
what you have done for them? How does a person's gratitude
affect what you will do for them in the future?

1 Chronicles 29:11-1 contains a wonderful truth: *"Thine, O
LORD, is the greatness, and the power, and the glory, and the
victory, and the majesty: for all that is in the heaven and in the earth
is thine; thine is the kingdom, O LORD, and thou art exalted as
head above all.*

*"Both riches and honour come of thee, and thou reignest over all;
and in thine hand is power and might; and in thine hand it is to*

make great, and to give strength unto all. Now therefore, our God,
we thank thee, and praise thy glorious name."

The truth is, that if we want to receive blessings from the
Lord– whether physical, mental or spiritual – the first step is
to show genuine gratitude for the things we already have and
for the things we hope to receive in the future. It makes only
logical sense that the closer we live to God (from whom all
riches flow), the more we will receive of those riches. "For it is
your Father's good pleasure to give you the kingdom" (Luke
12: 32). and we draw nigh to the Father through intense
gratitude, grounded in His Son Jesus Christ. If all you had to
be grateful for was the gift of His Son, then that would be more
than enough! Ponder on that fact for a moment!

Jesus, our great Exemplar, showed gratitude in all things.
Before he fed the multitudes with the meager loaves and
fishes, He gave thanks to His Father. When He raised Lazarus
from the dead, he said, "Father I thank thee that thou hast
heard me" (John 11:41). He even found something to be
grateful for when people rejected His message. "Jesus rejoiced
in spirit, and said, I thank thee, O Father, Lord of heaven and
earth, that thou hast hid these things from the wise and
prudent, and hast revealed them unto babes" (Luke 10: 21).

Start today and think of ways that you can show more
gratitude to God for His blessings and even your challenges.
Here are a few ideas to get you started. I'm sure you'll think of
more.

- Spend as much time thanking the Lord for an answer to prayer as you spent pleading for Him to give it to you.
- Offer one prayer a day that is nothing but a prayer of gratitude. Don't ask for anything, don't complain, just thank Him!
- Keep a gratitude journal of things that you are grateful for and write in it every day. When you're disappointed, feel like giving up, or just need a lift go back and read this journal.
- When other people do things for you, thank them and thank the Lord for bringing them into your life.
- While you're doing automatic tasks that don't require your higher mental abilities (like washing dishes, mowing the lawn, etc.) count your blessings. List them in your mind.
- Thank the Lord in advance for the things you know He'll do for you in the future.
- In any difficult situation, look for the good. Laced within every negative event is an equal and opposite good. You will find it if you thankfully look for it!

"Give thanks always for all things unto God and the Father in the name of our Lord Jesus Christ" - Ephesians 5:20

Are You Burying Your Talent

In Jesus' classic parable of the talents, the slothful servant who was given one talent hid his talent in the earth while his comrades doubled theirs from two to four and five to ten. When this servant's master came, he had done nothing with his talent. The servant answered his master, "I was afraid, and went and hid thy talent in the earth; lo there thou hast what is thine." As a result of his slothfulness, this servant was sorely punished and the one talent he had was given to the one who had ten.

Why did this servant hide his talent? What one emotion resulted in his punishment? Fear! He was afraid of what his master would do to him if he lost what he had given him. So rather than use it wisely, he hid it.

Many times the Lord opens doors of opportunity for us to develop and grow, but along with those doors come opposition. As the American Patriot Thomas Paine observed, "we have this consolation with us, that the harder the conflict, the more glorious the triumph. What we obtain too cheap, we esteem too lightly; 'tis dearness only that gives everything its value. Heaven knows how to put a proper price upon its goods."

That "price" is what makes many of us shrink back in fear and refuse to press forward. Many misread the "price" – the opposition attached to the opportunity – as the Lord telling them not to proceed in that direction. This may not be the case. If you have a strong desire to move in a certain direction, but you are uncertain about pursuing that desire, follow these 3 simple steps.

Step 1: Examine Your Desires

Ask yourself the following questions:

- Is this a righteous desire? Is it in line with the scriptures – the revealed word of God?
- Is my desire born of vain ambition? Or is it a desire to improve, to grow, to learn, to serve, and/or to make the world a better place?
- Is my hesitance to pursue my desires a result of fear? Am I afraid the Lord won't provide the means? Am I afraid of what other people might think? Am I afraid of failure? Am I afraid that I might appear foolish? Am I afraid that my feelings might get hurt?
- Do I know beyond doubt that the course I desire to pursue is the one God wants for me?

Step 2: Seek Confirmation

Anytime you have a desire or feeling that you should pursue a course, but you are uncertain or fearful, go to the Lord and seek a confirmation to learn whether your course is correct. Study it out in your mind, decide upon the best path to follow and then ask the Lord if it is right. Pray and perhaps fast about the situation. If you feel a feeling of love, joy, warmth and peace about your decision, then you know it is right. If you feel darkness, doubt, or confusion, then it is not the course for you. Once you have a confirmation, you have a foundation on which to build. You can say as the psalmist, "The Lord is on my side; I will not fear: what can man do unto me?" (Ps. 118: 6)

Step 3: Press Forward in Faith

Just because you now have a confirmation, doesn't mean you will not face opposition. Anchor yourself to God's plan for you – the confirmation you received. Have faith that no matter what the odds or the obstacles, God will open a way for you to proceed.

As Ecclesiastes 7:18 says, "It is good that thou shouldest take hold of this; yea, also from this withdraw not thine hand: for he that feareth God shall come forth of them all." Do not let obstacles, distractions or the day-to-day busyness of life cause you to withdraw your hand from the path God has laid out for you. As Joseph admonished his brothers, "See that ye fall not out by the way" (Genesis 45:24).

It may take time for the seed you plant today to become the tree God intends. Most goals that are worth accomplishing take time because they require that you obtain knowledge, experience, associations, and wisdom that you may now lack. Give God time to nourish and grow the seed. Do not rip it out in a few weeks, months or even years if it does not materialize. Give God time. "To everything there is a season, and a time to every purpose under heaven" (Ecclesiastes 3:1). We do not reap at the same time that we sow.

Think of Abraham when he was asked to sacrifice his son Isaac. The ram in the thicket did not appear until the very last moment as Abraham had the knife raised to slay his son. So also, we may be called to walk in faith until the very brink before the Lord delivers us. He's teaching us to trust in His timing and how to walk through darkness by the light of faith.

Trust the Lord when He has given you directions for he says to all those who follow Him, "Fear thou not; for I am with thee: be not dismayed; for I am thy God: I will strengthen thee; yea, I will help thee; yea, I will uphold thee with the right hand of my righteousness" (Isaiah 41:10).

The Faith to Forgive

Have you ever been betrayed by someone you trusted?
Someone you loved and counted on? Maybe that person
intentionally hurt you or maybe they just made a poor choice
that wreaked havoc on your life. At times we may feel as if
we've forgiven and moved on, but when we bump up against
the ramifications of another's acts, old feelings can re-emerge
— indicating that we have not completely forgiven after all.

Think of Joseph who was sold into slavery by his brothers.
They hated him, threw him into a pit, wanted to kill him, but
then enterprising Judah decided that they should sell him to
slave traders and turn a profit instead. When Joseph's
brothers finally caught up with him many years later, his
travels had brought him to the 2nd highest position in all of
Egypt. Only Pharaoh held more power and authority than
Joseph. But when Joseph revealed his identity to his brothers,
it was evident that he had forgiven them and saw the good in
the events of his life. He said, "Be not grieved, nor angry with
yourselves, that ye sold me hither: for God did send me before
you to preserve life. For these two years hath the famine been
in the land: and yet there are five years, in the which there
shall neither be earing nor harvest. And God sent me before
you to preserve you posterity in the earth, and to save your
lives by a great deliverance. So now it was not you that sent
me hither, but God: and he hath made me a father to Pharaoh,
and lord of all his house and a ruler throughout all the land of
Egypt." (Genesis 45:8)

What perspective and faith Joseph had! He wasn't bitter in
the least. Everything in his life up to that point indicates that

he never held a grudge – even when he was thrown into prison and stayed there for years. He always found the good and rose to the top in whatever circumstance he was placed. We can learn a great lesson from Joseph that we can apply to our own hardships. We can look for the good and see how God can use us in our current circumstances.

The following are some questions that we can ask ourselves when enduring adversity caused by others' poor choices:

· What would I choose to do now, in this given set of circumstances, that I may not have had the courage or willingness to do had I not come to this place?
· What have I learned from this experience? How is it making me a better person?
· How can knowing that God will make lemonade from this lemon, help me be more forgiving of the person whose choices have brought me here?
· What new people are a part of my life due to this path that I am traveling? How are these people improving my life? What can I learn from them?
· How is this experience enabling me to serve others with greater love and compassion?
· What options are now open to me that were not available before?
· How has my faith in God grown as a result of this?
· How is God using my adversity to bless others?

Having faith that God will make even your worst experiences work together for your good gives you the ability to forgive those who have harmed you. After all, it is the garden gate of our own little Gethsemanes that leads us to influential people, trains us, and gives us the opportunity to grow and develop the skills we need to become all that God knows we can be. Have you ever considered that the person who has harmed you was put in your life *because* God knew s/he would betray you and lead you on the path you needed to travel? Perhaps Joseph's brothers were chosen to be his siblings *because* God knew they could be counted on to betray him and thus set him on the path to save all of Egypt and future Israel! That's quite a thought to consider, isn't it!?

The Symbols of Christ at Christmas and All Year Through

At the Christmas season, our hearts turn to the Christ-child born in Bethlehem over 2,000 years ago. In its tinsel and trappings, even in this commercial age, the symbols of Christ remain. The Christmas tree, an evergreen, signifies the everlasting life afforded us through Jesus Christ. The star atop our tree represents that star which led the wise men to Bethlehem so long ago. The lights on our trees and the candles aglow remind us that Jesus is the Light of the World and that we too should carry His light to others by being a bright city set on a hill and a candlestick lit with His flame.

The candy cane typifies the shepherds abiding in the fields by night and the Good Shepherd whom they sought upon the angels' command. The spices in our cookies, pies and cakes are reminiscent of the spices brought to Him at His birth and those used in His burial by the women who loved Him.

The hanging mistletoe is one of the few plants that stays green in winter and continues to bear fruit when all the world is dead. Its greenery is symbolic of Christ who conquered death and now rules and reigns forever on high.

The presents we share at Christmas signify the gift our Heavenly Father gave to us of His Only Begotten Son and the gift that Christ gave us on Calvary's hill. His love that perme-ates the Christmas season engenders the feeling that because we have been given much we too must give.

The symbols of modern-day Christmas that point us back in time toward Christ are akin to the symbols that pointed ancient Israel forward toward Him. Like the children of Israel, we could benefit from the reminders of symbolism. Their sacrifices of unblemished first-born male lambs pointed forward to the sacrifice of the Lamb of God. When the poison-ous serpents in the wilderness bit the children of Israel, Moses lifted up a brass serpent on a pole. Those who looked lived; those who were too stubborn did not. Moses was pointing their minds forward toward Christ who would later be lifted up on the cross at Calvary – His life and mission in stark healing contrast to that old serpent the devil who introduced sin and death into this world.

As we read of Abraham and his heart-wrenching willingness to sacrifice his only son Isaac, our heart breaks for our Father in Heaven and His Son Jesus for whom no ram in the thicket would be provided. The emblems of the sacrament point us to the Savior's flesh and blood that He willingly gave on our behalf.

Symbolism is the sublime language of God. I heard someone say once "Jesus is the Master Teacher. The universe is His classroom and His curriculum is the Atonement." All things point to Christ. The universe is rich with His symbolism. The rising and setting sun and the cycle of seasons remind us of the birth, death and resurrection of the Savior and that one day because of Him, we will live again beyond the grave. The earth's annual revolution around the sun shows that if we too wish order and harmony in our lives they must revolve around the Son of God.

The flowers that droop at night and raise their heads to follow the sun in the morning symbolize our rebirth as we look to Christ and follow Him. The butterfly emerging from the caterpillar's cocoon typifies not only a universal resurrection, but also the miraculous transformation that Christ makes in the life of one repentant sinner.

All things denote there is a God, but even more specifically that He gave His Only Begotten Son that whosoever believeth in Him might not perish but might have everlasting life (John 3:16).

May our hearts turn to Christ this Christmas season and all year through as we look for the symbols of Him in the world around us and celebrate His life, His love and the blessings we have because of Him.

Sailing Ships with the Spirit of Christmas

Every year our family hosts a big Christmas party. It's one of the few occasions our extended family and long-time family-friends get together to enjoy each other's company. It's a family tradition we've kept for over 20 years, and one I hope our children continue long after we're gone. At the close of the evening as my Uncle Bob was singing *Amazing Grace* and then *Beulah Land*, I reflected on how evenings like this are a taste of heaven here on earth. This surely must be what heaven will be like with all of us together in the Spirit of Christmas. For it is that Spirit that is Christ's perfect love that takes on almost tangible proportions at this time of year, but which will be all encompassing in the hereafter. As I was carried away in contemplation, a stray thought entered my mind that made me shudder. How sad it would be to spend eternity separated from any single one of these precious souls. How hard it would be to have even one empty seat in those celestial realms! The thought filled me with sadness – a homesickness that is hard to put into words.

I am reminded of a story from the New Testament. In Acts chapter 27, the Apostle Paul had been taken prisoner and was being conducted to Rome via ship. Great storms arose and an angel came to Paul in the night, standing by him and said, "Fear not Paul...God hath given thee all them that sail with thee." Paul was thus able to both warn and comfort the others on the ship, "Be of good cheer: for there shall be no loss of any man's life among you, but of the ship."

Life is much like a perilous sea journey. But throughout the
storms of life, we are never left alone. Heavenly Father and our
Savior are with us. Also the Lord has given us all those who
sail with us. These are our family, our friends, our church
family, and all those who reach out and touch our lives for
good.

Our mortal bodies – our "ships" — may eventually be lost due
to death and disease, but the soul lives on. May we each do
everything within our power to bear witness of the Savior
each and every day of our lives so that those precious souls
who go with us on the journey will not be lost. May we each
teach, lift and build each other as we stand as witnesses of
Christ at all times and in all places, keeping the Spirit of
Christmas in our hearts each day and forever.

Index

About the Author

Marnie and her husband Greg
Pehrson are the parents of six
children and live in North Georgia
near Chattanooga, Tennessee.
Marnie is the founder of multi-denominational
SheLovesGod.com which hosts the annual SheLovesGod
Virtual Women's Conference the 3rd week of October each
year. She writes a weekly Bible study lesson which you may
subscribe to for free on the site. She has served in many
capacities within her church in presidencies of the women's
Relief Society and children's Primary organizations, and also
as a Sunday School teacher, pianist and family history
consultant.

Marnie is also an internet developer and consultant who
helps talented professionals deliver their message to the
online world. She is the creator of IdeaMarketers.com,
LocateACoach.com, PWGroup.com, BelieversAtWork.com, etc.
Throughout her sites, Marnie seeks to build resources that
help others discover, develop and utilize their God-given
talents.

Marnie welcomes reader comments and may be
reached at webmaster@SheLovesGod.com
or by calling 706-866-2295

Other Books by Marnie Pehrson

Lord, Are You Sure?
ISBN 0-9729750-0-4, 152 pages
A roadmap for understanding how Heavenly Father works in your life, helping you understand why certain problems keep repeating themselves, how to break the cycle and unlock the mystery of why you encounter challenges and roadblocks on roads you felt inspired to travel.

10 Steps to Fulfilling Your Divine Destiny: A Christian Woman's Guide to Learning & Living God's Plan for Her
ISBN 0-9676162-1-2, 124 pages
Have you ever said to yourself, "I'd love to do great things with my life, but I'm just too busy, too untalented, too ordinary, too afraid, too anything but extraordinary"? Inside this book you'll learn how to reach your full God-given potential.

Journal/Workbook Companion for 10 Steps to Fulfilling Your Divine Destiny: A Christian Woman's Guide to Learning & Living God's Plan for Her
ISBN 0-9676162-2-0, 220 pages

Packets of Sunlight for Christian Parents
Compiled by: Marnie L. Pehrson
ISBN 0-9676162-4-7, 144 pages, paperback
Brighten your day with inspiration for parents of tots to teens!

Packets of Sunlight for American Patriots
Compiled by: Marnie L. Pehrson
ISBN 0-9676162-3-9, 108 pages, paperback
Let the founding fathers, reignite your love for freedom!

Rebecca's Reveries

Historical Fiction
by Marnie L. Pehrson
ISBN 0-9729750-2-0, 224 pages, paperback
Rebecca Marchant had led a sheltered life until she found
herself inexplicably drawn to the home of her father's youth.
Surrounded by the historical landscape of the Chickamauga
Battlefield in Georgia Rebecca finds herself plagued by
haunting dreams and vivid visions of Civil War events. As
Rebecca walks a mile in another girl's moccasins through her
visions and dreams she learns about compassion, forgiveness,
temptation and the power of true love. More information at
http://www.pwgroup.com/reveries/

The Patriot Wore Petticoats

Historical Fiction, Scheduled for Release in 2004
by Marnie L. Pehrson
Daring "Dicey" Langston, the bold and reckless rider and
expert shot, saves her family and an entire village during the
American Revolution. Having faced British soldiers, rushing
swollen rivers, the "Bloody Scouts," and the barrel of a loaded
pistol, nothing had quite prepared this valiant heroine for the
heart-pounding exhilaration she'd find in the arms of one
brave Patriot. Based on a true story about the author's fourth
great-grandmother. Learn more at www.DiceyLangston.com

To order call 800-524-2307 or visit www.SheLovesGod.com/bookstore

www.ingramcontent.com/pod-product-compliance
Lightning Source LLC
Chambersburg PA
CBHW030011110426
42741CB00032B/275